Rewarding Your Sales Force

Rewarding Your Sales Force

W. G. RYCKMAN

KOGAN PAGE

The male pronoun has been used throughout this book. This stems from a desire to avoid ugly and cumbersome language, and no discrimination, prejudice or bias is intended.

First published in the United States of America in 1986 by
Probus Publishing Company, Chicago, Illinois
ISBN 0–917253–38–8
Library of Congress Catalog Card Number: 85–30058

First published in Great Britain in 1989 by
Kogan Page Ltd,
120 Pentonville Rd, London N1 9JN
Typeset by J&L Composition Ltd., Filey, North Yorkshire.
Printed and bound in Great Britain

British Library Cataloguing in Publication Data
Ryckman, W. G.
[Compensating your sales force] Rewarding your sales force.
1. Salesmen. Incentive schemes. Design
I. Title
658.3′225

ISBN 1–85091–936–4

CONTENTS

PREFACE

This book is about rewards for sales forces. It is written for sales managers up the line, from branch level to corporate executives.

A well-designed reward scheme for salesmen has two main objectives:

1. To reward salesmen so that their earnings will bear a direct relationship to the value of their contributions to the company.
2. To enable the company to stimulate its salesmen and to focus their efforts in directions that will profit them while helping the company meet its sales objectives.

That's all there is to it. To assist you in the development or the restructuring of your company's reward scheme we will explore various methods of paying salesmen, showing the strengths and weaknesses of each. We will discuss territories, targets, salesmen's expenses, contests and policy decisions management must make.

It is my hope that you will find helpful suggestions in the book. Good luck to you and good selling.

W.G. Ryckman

INTRODUCTION

Before getting into the book proper, I would like to outline briefly my view of the basic relationship between salesmen and their bosses — the several layers of management that to a large extent control their destinies. To my way of thinking, salesmen and management are interdependent; one cannot exist without the other. Each relies on the other to achieve goals, corporate goals, on the one hand, and personal goals for the individual salesmen, on the other. What is good for the salesman should be good for the company and vice versa.

In reading some of the literature on the subject it becomes apparent that not everyone agrees with my attitude. Management and salesmen are often cast in the roles of adversaries with opposing objectives. I cannot accept this approach. Salesmen rely on their earnings to support their families and themselves; companies could not exist without an efficient means of distributing their goods. Neither can survive without the other.

Naturally, companies feel they have the right to direct and control the activities of their representatives, and salesmen feel they have a right to equitable treatment. I do not find any area in such a relationship that could result in a basic difference between the two parties.

Each understanding the other's needs is essential, as is mutual trust and respect. Companies succeed because their workers are successful; salesmen are successful when the company supports them, that is, makes it possible for them to achieve their goals provided they work toward them conscientiously and in accordance with company policies.

Much of what I have to say in the book is coloured by this attitude. I am on the side of the salesman; at the same time I am on the side of the company. I do not find any conflict or inconsistency in my stance.

So much for an introduction. Now, let's get on with it.

Footnote: British Edition

Throughout this book examples are given of commission plans. It should be noted that these are only given as indicative of the specific points being made, and each sales manager will need to produce his own plan to meet his own organization's particular needs. The calculations shown generally assume a sales professional earning of the order of £25,000 a year; such as is, for example, the case in the office equipment field. On the other hand, there are many sales forces, in other industries, which are paid at rates considerably below this. The sales managers in these cases will need to adjust the figures accordingly. We make no apology, though, for using the example of the highest achievers, at least in reward terms, where that is what this book is all about!

Chapter 1

REWARD SCHEMES—A MANAGER'S PERSPECTIVE

Reward schemes for salesmen are designed to accomplish several objectives. Among these are: to assist the company in meeting its sales projections, to bring the earnings of the sale force to desired levels and to reward each individual salesman in direct proportion to his efforts and performance.

The objectives enumerated are closely interrelated; one cannot be considered while the others are ignored. Mutual interdependency, we might call it. To accomplish these worthy goals a scheme should be sound, equitable, as simple as possible and flexible.

Let's start by discussing corporate sales objectives. No two companies will have identical sales goals. The entrenched sales leader strives to hold his substantial share of market; a smaller competitor attempts to wrest a few points of market share from him. The large national company desires greater penetration in its districts; the smaller regional company engages in an expansion programme to enter new sales markets.

To refine sales objectives even further we can suppose that to one company, increasing gross sales is a prime consideration. It may plan for a growth rate of 20 per cent in each of the next five years. Another organization that is more concerned with profitability might seek to refine the mix of its products, emphasizing those with the larger gross margins.

Companies have other goals allied to, but not directly connected with, the primary aim of selling their goods or services. New accounts may be a necessity, especially when a company changes from a skim to a penetration policy in a territory.

In some industries it is essential to expend time and effort in missionary work, from which no immediate reward is possible but sales could benefit substantially in the future. For example, a health care company might develop a new toothpaste and a toothbrush both especially designed to serve the needs of eight- to twelve-year-old children. Its merchandisers would distribute thousands of samples to dentists, expecting them to be passed on to the parents of young patients making their regular check-up visits. Sales generated by these free samples might reach imposing levels in the future if the dentists have been convinced of the value of the products.

Rapidly expanding companies are constantly opening new territories. Some unfortunate organizations discover that reimbursed expenses of salesmen are getting out of line and more control over them is needed. Still others, even less fortunate, discover an alarming increase in bad debts written off, and must rely on the sales force to help in correcting the situation.

A well-designed and well-administered reward scheme can be an important tool that, properly used, will provide invaluable assistance to a company in achieving its objectives, whatever they are. The reward scheme has other uses, as well.

It is a major factor in the maintenance and development of a sales force. A company succeeds or fails based on the performance of its salesmen, and the motivation and morale of these representatives are to a considerable extent influenced by the reward scheme adopted by the company. A secure sales force, comfortable in its role and satisfied with its earnings will be productive; a force inequitably paid under a poorly designed and administered reward scheme will not function in a manner satisfactory to its employer, nor will it be content with its earnings.

Sales managers are constantly looking for men and women to add to their sales forces. Each company has its own standards to control hiring practices. Among the qualities most frequently considered are ability, background, education, experience and in some instances age.

The reward scheme can be either a strong force in attracting the right type of person to the company or, conversely, an equally strong deterrent from joining a sales force. Added to this is the ever-present fear of the competition. If the company's scheme is not competitive with the industry in which the company operates, the sales manager starts out with the odds stacked against him. He will be unable to hire the people he wants and must make do with the misfits and leavings of his competitors.

Of equal if not greater importance to the sales manager is the necessity to retain personnel of proven ability. Salesmen will stay on the job if they are paid fairly and treated like human beings. Who can blame an individual for leaving one company for another that will pay him 20 per cent more for similar work? Consider the cost of losing an experienced salesman. A replacement must first be found. He must be trained. Weeks or months must pass before he gains familiarity with the territory to which he is assigned and the idiosyncrasies of each buyer with whom he will deal.

In the meantime the man he replaces will be doing everything in his power to lure company customers to his new employer, your competitor. Losing a good salesman is an expensive proposition and the cost is even more difficult to bear when the loss is due to a failure either in the company reward scheme or its administration.

The company should expect that a well-designed reward scheme will encourage the sales force to achieve at least adequate sales performance. It should stimulate the men and women to do better for themselves. If this is accomplished, the company will benefit equally.

Finally, the plan should be so structured that performance is rewarded equitably. Reward schemes should relate payment with performance — no freeloaders, no exploited 'nice guys'. Even a few individuals paid more than they are worth will wreck an organization, and the loyal, good fellows who are doing a creditable job will sooner or later move on to fresher fields and greener pastures.

And don't forget, there are many aspects of performance; sales production is highly important, of course, but other contributions are valuable, as well. Training new men, helping out in a crisis, loyally supporting the company, willingness to listen to and back the boss are all important in any organization. Superior contribution in these areas should be recognized and rewarded.

It is easy to measure the sales production of a salesman. You are dealing with a tangible, finite matter and the proper compensation for performance is not difficult to determine. Yet, when you attempt to reward a man for the intangible services he renders the organization, you encounter substantial difficulties. Judgements must be mainly subjective on the part of management and the mettle of a sales manager is severely tested when he must decide on the value of a man's contribution in these areas. However, reward them he must if he expects his organization to perform smoothly and effectively.

A number of authorities on the subject of salesmen's rewards have expressed the opinion that a sales manager should strive to pay his men and women as little as possible and still keep them willing to do their jobs. In other words, don't pay a penny more than you have to. Some of the pundits strike a high tone in defending such a stand. They talk of seducing people to work for money, contending their motivation should stem from the satisfaction of achievement on the job.

We have looked at reward schemes through the eyes of an employer, the company. Now let us consider how the salesman regards them.

Sales managers advance from the ranks of salesmen and memories of their early days should be vivid enough to remind them of their hopes and aspirations when they sold for a living. A salesman's attitude has not changed much in the intervening years. What does he want from his job as far as money is concerned?

First of all he expects fair payment for his performance. What is fair? Fair from whose point of view? Who says anything in this imperfect world of ours must be fair? It isn't a very useful word to use when describing rewards.

What the salesman has in mind when he uses the word is that he should receive payment that is in line with that offered by the competition and commensurate with the quality of the job he does. If he sells in high volume, he feels entitled to high earnings; if he spends time training new men, doing missionary work, making service calls, he should be recompensed for those activities.

He looks for simplicity in a scheme; he wants to understand it fully and not run into unusual provisions that, to his mind, have been introduced for the sole purpose of denying him what is rightfully his.

He likes a plan that supplies him with a steady income at least on a minimum level to help him over occasional spells of small commission earnings.

Fair is not the only sticky word. Add another — contribution. How is contribution measured and evaluated? How many points for sales volume, training, attitude and all the other traits good salesmen are expected to exhibit? Join considerations of contribution with those of fairness as related to compensation and you compound the problem.

A salesman wants a scheme to be flexible. Some territories are more difficult to cover than others, some are rich, others comparatively poor. Schemes should have the resilience to reward for such differences that are out of a salesman's control.

Last, but certainly not least, is a salesman's conviction that any scheme should provide an opportunity for him to improve his status: still higher earnings, a clear road to promotion.

How do these salesmen's objectives relate to company goals? There should be, and in fact there are, no real areas of conflict. In the best of all possible worlds what is good for a salesman should be good for his company. It doesn't always work out that way in details, but differences should not be great provided both sides are activated by a sense of equity and good will.

The company should appreciate the need for flexibility. Age of a man or woman, years of service with the company and past contribution are important factors that should not be ignored. Too much flexibility can be a handicap, too. A scheme unique to every man would result in chaos. Basically, a standard scheme is desirable, but the various elements of it should be subject to adjustment for special circumstances.

Above all, the scheme any company adopts should be in line with the competition as regards total compensation. Except for compelling reasons to the contrary, a company would not structure its scheme so that the reward would be 25 per cent above or below its leading competitors in the field. In addition, a scheme should be compatible with a company's ability to pay.

A final word. Once a company has determined the average level of reward to be earned by its men, or in a large organization by each class of salesmen, the prime consideration should be the total amount paid, not on what basis it is paid. No matter how well a scheme is designed, it is doomed to failure unless total reward paid is competitive in the industry and represents equitable remuneration for services rendered.

The chart labelled 'Attitudes toward a Reward Scheme' recapitulates the points that have been made about the desirable elements of a reward scheme. The viewpoints of the salesman have been contrasted with those of the company and it should be a surprise to no one that the interests of both parties are in almost every case entirely compatible. What is good for the salesman is good for the company. There can be no fundamental conflict between men and management in a well-run organization. That is a good thought to keep in mind as you develop a reward scheme for your sales force.

There are a number of ways in which a sales force can be rewarded, ranging from salary to fringe benefits and perks. Each method can be employed to aid a company in achieving a desired result. Each has strengths peculiar to it, but none is an unmixed blessing. Unfavourable as well as favourable elements are implicit in each method of payment. In the following chapters we will discuss and analyse the most prevalent means of rewarding salesmen.

Attitudes toward a Reward Scheme

Salesmen look for	Company's attitude
Adequate income for adequate performance	No conflict, no argument on this point
Superior income for superior performance	None here either
Incentives for special achievement	All but a few reactionary companies agree.
A base of fixed income for security purposes	Many companies agree, but some cannot afford a fixed expense like salary. In certain industries compensation historically has ranged from 100 per cent salary to 100 per cent commission. Company attitude will depend on circumstances peculiar to it.
At least primary fringe benefits	No argument here, but not all companies can afford full range
Opportunity for advancement, promotion	As much to the company's advantage as the salesman's
A yardstick to measure performance	Equally important for the company to measure performance
Equitable treatment for all salesmen. Pay based on performance — no free loaders, no favouritism or exploitation	
A sense of security through the knowledge he is respected and	

Attitudes toward a Reward Scheme *(continued)*

Salesmen look for	Company's attitude
regarded as a human being who is important to the company	Equally important to the employer
Flexibility in a plan, sensitivity to changing conditions	Just as important to the company, which must rely on the morale of its sales force. The sense of security and well-being of a sales force pay many bonuses to an employer.
Simplicity — easy to understand	Equally important to a company
	The company agrees — the simpler the plan, the easier and cheaper to administer it

Hints to Sales Managers

- Be sensitive to the needs and aspirations of your salesmen.
- Remember that just as you control their success, so also do they control yours.
- In your relationships with your sales force there is no substitute for straight dealing and equity.
- Be aware that the best reward scheme is the one that most accurately measures and rewards the performance of a salesman.
- Utilize your reward scheme as a tool to aid you in meeting as many company objectives as possible.
- Above all, never lose sight of the fact that performance and earnings should go hand-in-hand.
- Realize that the company and the sales force are not adversaries, but partners with nearly identical goals.

Chapter 2

SALARY

A straight salary payroll is by far the easiest for the employer to handle. Deductions for tax and national insurance, as well as other items such as pension contributions, are easily calculated and the work load is reduced to punching a few computer keys and writing a cheque once or twice a month.

In many industries this method of compensation is generally used and there is always an overriding reason for choosing a salary plan. Let us look at a few businesses taking the salary route and certain types of selling best rewarded by salary.

Highly Seasonal Industries

Consider a company, the major source of whose business is the sale of tennis rackets. The main sales period is the lead up to the spring and salesmen spend the balance of the year developing new accounts.

Under a salary plan, a salesman's income will be spread evenly over the year whereas if he were on commission he would be subject to a long famine between short-team feasts. The company is obligated for fixed expenses during periods of low sales but the payment of regular salary effectively assures retention of salesmen.

High-Tech Industries

Salesmen for companies in this field are usually men and women of high calibre — well educated, highly trained and self-motivated. Often they have degrees in electrical or mechanical engineering, chemistry or other sciences. These individuals must be categorized as sales engineers. They spend large segments of time advising customers, working on installation of products and training users.

Companies believe, and with reason, that representatives of this type do not require incentive pay as motivation to perform their duties. Salary, provided it is commensurate with contribution, is the ideal method of payment. It gives the employer full control over the activities of its sales force and the individual develops a sense of belonging to and importance in the company.

Trade Salesmen

This category includes those engaged in the distribution of products such as food and wearing clothes who do little or no creative selling. Markets are well defined and the salesman does not appreciably influence either the sizes of orders or the number of customers in his territory. In fact, he is often referred to as an 'order taker'.

Company advertising and promotion develop sales more effectively than the salesman. Other than taking orders, about all he can contribute is to set up displays and restock shelves. Both the company and the representative look at such a job as best compensated by salary.

Route Salesmen

Beer and soft drink salesmen as well as bread and milk delivery drivers are normally paid by salary. There is little they can do to increase sales or add customers on their routes, so a reward scheme involving incentives would not be of value either to the salesman or the company.

Missionary and Educational Salesmen

This type of salesperson does little direct selling to the company's ultimate customers. His job is to encourage retailers to buy his company's products from the wholesaler or other organization through which it sells. Thus, a drug manufacturer's missionary force would urge chemists to order that firm's products from its wholesaler.

This kind of selling, if it can be called that, is low key and tangible results of missionary efforts are difficult to measure. There appears to be no alternative to the payment of salary to individuals employed in work of this sort.

Group Selling

In some manufacturing businesses selling requires a group effort involving a field man who generates interest in a product (often machinery, a complicated fabricated part or a raw material processed to rigid specifications), factory technicians, development engineers, managers who set prices and terms, installers and trainers at the customer's plant. When business is done in this fashion, many companies pay straight salaries to all their employees involved in the selling process. No other way of paying equitable compensation is practical. Salary paid to the different classifications of employees should be commensurate with the value of the services performed.

Many selling jobs other than those enumerated are rewarded by salary. For some this method of payment is the best, for others a different payment base might be substantially superior. When opening a new business, management should make a complete analysis of the disadvantages as well as the advantages implicit in a salary plan. When considering a change to salaried salesmen, an ongoing business should make an even more exhaustive study. There are strengths in salary plans, but there are weaknesses as well — for the employer as well as individual salesmen.

Salaried salesmen appreciate the security of a regular income. Orders seldom flow evenly and it is comforting to know a regular income will be received when sales production has fallen off during a slack period.

The security that comes hand in hand with salary is a strong factor in lowering turnover in a sales force. Management approves this aspect of a salary plan. It is not as happy, however, with the realization that the salary tends to keep weak, unproductive men on the payroll long after they would have disappeared had they been paid by commissions on sales made. The sales manager knows how difficult it is to terminate a salaried employee; eliminating misfits is one of his least pleasant duties.

Salary rewards are especially effective when a balanced effort is required of a salesman. Generation of sales might be his primary responsibility, but other important duties such as missionary calls, training new men, service work and so forth usually are required of him. The sales manager can require attention to these peripheral duties of a salaried man since he draws part of his salary for performing them. Control over a sales force is not always easy to maintain, but the ability to control salary is a major tool in the hands of a sales manager.

From a salesman's point of view, the security that accompanies a salary is important and so also is the sense of belonging that comes with it. A salaried person feels he works for the company; a commission man may feel he is in business for himself and more often than not opposes any attempt to direct or control his activities. This problem is much less serious if the salesman is on salary. The distinction between the attitudes of salary and commission men may be mainly psychological, but it is nonetheless real.

A salaried sales force limping along under weak management can destroy an organization quickly and completely. Without a firm hand on the tiller, many salaried salesmen tend to disregard their responsibilities and declining sales inevitably result. Salary can effectively reward only when supervision is of high caliber and stimulating to men.

From management's perspective one of the greatest values of a salaried organization is the advantage it gives a company when it hires new men. A steady dependable income while learning a business is a great attraction to a potential employee. In addition to the tangible benefit, the new man feels that the company really considers him a valuable asset, one worthy of generous treatment.

Salary can also be a help when new territories are being opened. It would probably take some time before a salesman could exist on the commissions from sales, especially when several months elapse between order and delivery. The same is true when an entirely new generation of products is introduced and a number of experienced men are assigned to establish the line.

On the other hand, there are basic weaknesses inherent in paying salesmen a straight salary. Salary is a fixed cost. It does not fluctuate with sales volume. A company approves a salary schedule based on what it believes to be an accurate projection of sales for the year. Suppose an unexpected event occurs or the economic environment worsens and sales drop 30 per cent below expectations. Salary cost remains a constant, however, and selling costs rise to an unacceptable level. Not an enviable position for a company to be in.

On the other hand, sales might show an unusual and sustained increase. In that case the company will profit from the fixed nature of salary expense. Yet, how long will the sales force accept present salary rates in the light of substantially increased sales production? If rises are given, the next slump makes the problem even worse.

The chart below illustrates the effect on adjusted gross income when sales deviate from expectations and selling costs are fixed rather than variable expenses.

Sales	£100*	£130*	£70*
Cost of goods sold	80	104	56
Gross margin	20	26	14
Selling expenses	10	10	10
Adjusted gross margin	10	16	4

* All figures expressed in millions

In all three examples cost of goods sold is 80 per cent of sales. Selling expenses, consisting principally of salaries, remain at £10 million.

The effect of the fixed nature of selling expenses is readily apparent. When the company meets its projected sales volume of £100 million, the adjusted gross margin is 10 per cent of sales. With a 30 per cent increase in sales this figure jumps to £16 million, 12.3 per cent of sales. When sales drop 30 per cent the adjusted gross margin falls to £4 million, 5.7 per cent of sales.

Had selling expenses been a variable expense, say 10 per cent of sales, adjusted gross margin with the increased sales would have risen only £3 million and declined a like amount when sales volume fell. Thus the fixed nature of selling expenses added an extra £3 million to margins when sales increased and cost the company an additional £3 million when they fell.

Another complaint of employers about the straight salary method of compensation is that it does not supply sufficient incentive to the salesmen to increase production. A man might be quite content with his earnings as they are. Why should he work harder for the company when he will derive no direct benefit from the increased effort? If he expended more energy his salary might be increased in the future, but it's a big if and how much of a rise could he expect anyway?

A properly administered salary plan makes frequent adjustments necessary. If too infrequent or niggardly, the effect would be to demotivate the sales force. Conversely, if changes are made too often the salary becomes almost the same as commission with one important difference. Commissions rise in good times and fall in a recession. No problem arises when salaries are increased, but what sales manager enjoys the prospect of having to cut salaries and at the same time keep his salesmen motivated?

A fixed commission scale is one thing, adjustable salaries quite another. Very often rises are perceived by the sales force as arbitrary and dictated by expediency. Capable management is essential and even so, problems will inevitably arise.

In the eyes of many men, the old timers get paid too much, as do the weak sisters that management is too soft-hearted to fire. The young tigers know they are underpaid. The feeling builds that time on the job and old pals in management have more influence in setting salary levels than production does. All this leads to frustration and frustration inhibits selling.

One final note. Employing a salaried sales force when launching a new business is not recommended if financial resources are limited. Salary payments march along inexorably, pound after pound, while sales may at first be disappointingly slow. Analyse your bank balance and estimate cash flow in an ultraconservative manner before obligating yourself to a salaried sales force.

The chart labelled 'Analysis of Straight Salary Reward Scheme' itemizes the assets and liabilities associated with salary compensation of salesmen. Salary plans are neither all good nor all bad. Company circumstances and method of doing business must be taken into account before a salary plan is adopted or rejected.

Analysis of Straight Salary Reward Schemes

From salesman's viewpoint	From company's viewpoint
STRENGTHS	
Simple, uncomplicated Stablility of income Job security enhanced Sense of belonging to organization	Simple, easy to administer Reduces turnover in sales force Increases authority of sales manager in controlling salesmen Makes it easier for management to secure cooperation of men An effective tool when: — Hiring new men — Introducing new product line — Business is highly seasonal — Large percentage of salesmen's time is spent in missionary or educational work — Selling requires group effort — Business is highly technical in nature and sales force is of extremely high calibre — Selling is mainly order taking — Sales management is of proven superior ability
WEAKNESSES	
Lack of incentive to excel, increase production Salary increases seen as too small, too late, not based on performance but on favouritism Old timers, weak sisters tend to be overpaid Production leaders often underpaid	Fixed expense, difficult to cut Tends to keep inept on payroll When leadership (management) is weak there is little incentive to increase sales Frequent adjustments in salary are necessary, yet too many changes are as bad as too few Financially weak companies are often unable to bear the expense of salaried salesmen Requires excellent supervision, which is not always available

Hints to Sales Managers

- Check your company's finances. Can you afford salaried salesmen?
- Is your company's business cyclical in nature, especially sensitive to economic swings? If so, what effect could fixed selling costs have on your profits?
- Do any of your major competitors use a salary reward scheme? If not, why should you consider one?
- List your company's sales objectives. What will you gain by paying salary to your men? What will you lose?
- Make sure you explore the other methods of rewarding your men before you make any decision on a reward scheme.

Chapter 3

STRAIGHT COMMISSION

Paying commission has one great advantage over paying salary from the company's point of view. It is a variable expense rather than a fixed one. If sales are made, commission is paid — no sales, no commission. This keeps selling expenses strictly in line.

On the other hand, salary payments march inexorably on regardless of sales volume. Selling costs can get entirely out of hand, especially when sales are on a downward trend.

A commission pay plan has many other virtues. It is desirable for a company suffering a severe cash shortage since commission need not be paid until proceeds are received on a sale.

Generous commission rates can be a strong incentive to salesmen, an element of much less influence under a salary plan, and many organizations are successful because the sales force enjoys a liberal commission schedule. Commission-based compensation is favoured by many companies to which sales volume is of paramount importance and little activity is needed in such areas as missionary work or service requirements. In many cases sales volume written is the primary measure of the value of a man.

Some industries historically have taken the commission route. For example, the financial services industries, particularly life insurance, have often chosen this form of compensation. The reason for adopting the commission plan is readily apparent.

Consider an estate agent engaged in selling residential properties. He or she has only two major duties: to sell houses and to find new clients for his or her employer. Making a sale earns a portion of the commission payable; securing a sole agency from a client means a share of commission when anyone else sells the property.

A new car salesman for a dealer works the same way. His job is to sell cars. He is not asked to wash them when they are received or repair automobiles damaged in accidents.

The value of either person to his employer is easy to determine — what he has sold is what counts. Paying commission on sales is the only equitable way to reward such an individual.

The same method of payment is usually chosen when a large portion of the sales force is composed of part-timers or individuals who work an irregular schedule. In such cases, effective field supervision is not possible and control over selling activities is either weak or entirely lacking.

There is another group of men and women who are generally paid on a commission basis. Consider those employed in large numbers who sell their wares from house to house: brushes, household appliances, silver, cosmetics, kitchen appliances. Payment of salary would not be economically sound due to rapid turnover and lack of production on the part of many who are hired. Avon representatives are paid commission on sales. We are told there are 400,000 of them. Could any company afford to pay a salary to all those people?

Yet thousands of men and women earn substantial incomes through their efforts in door-to-door selling. They elect the freedom to work at their own pace that a commission base allows to the control over their activity inherent in a salary plan. Successful men and women in this area of selling are a special breed of people who take justifiable pride in their accomplishments.

I believe that we may correctly assume that a majority of people will work harder for sales when income depends on commission than when they are compensated by salary. I probably should modify that statement by adding that I refer to that group of men and women who are sufficiently self-motivated to want to better their social and economic status in life. Some people just won't respond to any stimulus, internal or external in origin. A salary that keeps a roof over their heads and groceries on the table suffices them. Commission compensation supplies no incentive to such individuals.

Fortunately, however, another segment of our working population, and a large one, welcomes the opportunity offered them in a selling job. They want to get ahead and to prosper, and a commission plan is the surest way for them to attain their goals.

Salary levels are to a large extent controlled by the overall performance of a company and the policies it operates under. The commission salesman, on the other hand, is master of his own fate. He can set his goals and rely on his initiative and ability to reach them. In doing so he is largely independent of the varying fortunes of his company.

This type of salesman requires more than motivation to enjoy success to the fullest extent. The outside commission salesman needs a strong sense of discipline, a trait not always found in salesmen. Even if his sales manager is the best in the business, the salesman spends most of his day on his own. He sets his own hours, his own schedules, he punches no time clock and his boss has little opportunity to check what he is doing.

Some people never learn how to discipline themselves, yet, without that ability jobs don't get done. An excuse can always be found not to undertake an unpleasant task. Commission salesmen lacking the ability to set their own standards as to work hours and level of dedication to the job will suffer unless an alert sales manager can act as their conscience. Alert, certainly, but the manager must be sensitive and perceptive too.

Even the best salesman has barren spells when his most earnest efforts produce few positive results. During periods of depressed earnings household expenses continue on their merry way and even the most positive man can begin to doubt his ability.

The sales manager must exert a strong supportive influence when he observes that a man is going through one of these periods. It is also a manager's responsibility, while recognizing the independent feelings of his men, to convince them that they really are a valuable part of the company and their contributions are fully appreciated.

The weaknesses of a straight commission method of reward management lie in the same area as the strengths of a salary plan. In like fashion the weaknesses of a salary plan are often the strengths associated with compensation by commission.

A major weakness in a commission plan is that it makes hiring new men difficult for a company, particularly when training requires a protracted period without pay. Likewise, assignment of experienced men to new or undeveloped territories can cause serious problems. No man wants to sacrifice a steady income earned in familiar surroundings, even for the greater potential of a new location, if his earnings will be sharply reduced for a period of several months or even longer.

These weaknesses in a commission plan are important ones for companies starting in business or those entering a programme of expansion into new areas.

Whereas salary makes it easier to control an employee's activities, payment of commission diminishes the sales manager's authority. It is difficult for him to require men to do missionary work or even to concentrate on certain products that are more profitable for the company.

In good times, commission men are inclined to skim their territory and ignore the necessity of developing new accounts for the future. Often salesmen will over-sell customers in order to make a higher commission. This practice can result in customer ill-will and returns.

In short, commission men may be more inclined to consider their own interests over those of the company. In combating this tendency, sales managers earn a good part of their keep. Each salesman is a different person. No general course of action a sales manager can take will be effective with all his men.

This fact points up the necessity for the manager to know all that is to be known about his sales force. A sales manager must lead and guide, and to accomplish these essential tasks he must be respected by his sales people.

This is the first time we have mentioned the word respect in this book. It is such an important word and relates to such a vital attribute of sales management that we'll spend a few paragraphs discussing the concept. This is a good spot to talk about the subject, as the sales manager needs the respect of the commission man more than any other type of salesman and the respect of that class of individual is the most difficult to win. Why?

First, because a salaried man realizes his superior is his boss and should be obeyed in order to progress in the company. A commission salesman is often loath to acknowledge anyone's authority over him. Second, because the commission man, being a strong, supremely self-confident individual, does not take kindly to control or anyone who attempts to exert it.

Yet if a sales manager is to be successful, he must be able to guide and direct his people. If he is not respected he cannot hope to achieve his aims. How does one gain respect?

I once knew rather well the president of a corporation that employed thousands of salesmen. He was a powerful man, a great salesman himself and a tenacious bulldog. He grabbed hold and never let go. Once I heard him say when speaking of his sales force, 'I don't care whether they like me or not, but I demand their respect.' How wrong he was. Nobody can secure respect by demand; it must be earned. In attempting to demand it my friend was no better than King Canute ordering the tide to halt its rise.

How does a sales manager earn respect? Here are the five basic factors I believe are involved in the process. Every sales manager should possess these traits.

Dependability

A sales manager's word must be his bond. No waffling, no shilly-shallying can be tolerated. Once a decision is made and announced that is it — no ifs, ands or buts. Promises are kept. It adds up to strength of character.

Support

A manager must support his or her sales force, backing them to the hilt when they are right, yet being equally firm in correcting them when they are wrong.

Honesty, Equity, a Sense of Fair Play

This trait implies no favouritism and equal justice for everyone. It also allows no half-truths, but requires complete and open disclosure. Telling it like it is, as the saying goes. Such an attitude begets trust, and without trust there can be no respect.

A Genuine Interest in People

The manager must have concern for employees and along with that, compassion when disciplinary action must be taken.

Mastery of the Job

No one can truly respect a bungler, even a well-intentioned one. Sales managers should be effective, in control of themselves as well as the organization. They must be strong, not reluctant to take action when it is called for and at all times decisive — not afraid to take a stand.

Rewards by Straight Commission

From salesman's viewpoint	From company's viewpoint
STRENGTHS	
Incentive to increase income	Commission is a variable, not a fixed, expense
Knowledge that he is master of his pay cheque — that he will be paid in direct proportion to his sales production	Selling expenses, as a function of sales are controllable — an advantage when cash is scarce
Knowledge that he is not dependent on company policy regarding rises	It is a strong incentive to salesmen to increase production
Knowledge that his earnings do not depend on profitability of the company	A good plan when securing orders is prime duty of salesmen
Knowledge that he can set his own goals and profit from meeting them	Excellent for part-timers
WEAKNESSES	
Lack of stable income causes hardship in slack times	Loss of control over sales force
Requires a high degree of discipline in financial matters — a quality not always found in salesmen	Diminished authority of sales manager
Lack of income as a new man or when opening a new territory	Leads to skimming in rich territories
Lack of feeling of belonging to organization	Leads to over-selling
	Leads to ignoring of duties other than selling

Rewards by Straight Commission ***(continued)***

From salesman's viewpoint	From company's viewpoint
	Salesmen inclined to place their own interests above those of company
	May lead to an adversary attitude between men and management

Hints to Sales Managers

- Pay by commission if you employ a large number of part-timers.
- Commission plans rely heavily on the incentive factor — make sure each salesman knows what successful selling can mean to him.
- Discover the key to each of your men's motivation and use it to help him achieve his full potential.
- *You* are the sales manager. Manage your men — don't let them manage you.
- Offer advice and guidance in financial management to your men.
- Above all, strive to earn the respect of every person in your organization.

Chapter 4

COMMISSION RATES

Historically commission has been paid on sales volume. On a fixed commission base, an established percentage of sales volume is paid to a salesman. Other plans call for increases in rate as volume increases. In still others, a regressive schedule decreases the rate as volume increases.

Fixed rate commission is easy to figure and administer. If the rate is 4 per cent, it stays at that percentage whether the salesman sells £20,000 or £200,000. The rate may be applied to turnover, gross margin, even unit sales — whatever base the company adopts.

A progressive commission rate accomplishes a major objective of most corporations: it provides a constant incentive to a sales force to do better for itself. Consider this example:

	Sales	*Commission rate*
Up to	£50,000	3%
From	£50,000 to £100,000	4%
Above	£100,000	5%

If a man's quota is £75,000, he would earn £2,500 if he hit it exactly, a composite rate of 3.33 per cent. If he sold £115,000, he would be paid £4,250, a composite rate of 3.7 per cent. Superior pay for superior performance. Such a programme makes sense. The more the company sells, the better it should do and the more the salesman sells, the greater should be his reward.

We must add a word of caution here, however. Salesmen are sharp, never forget that. If the rules allow a way to beat the system, the salesman will find it. He is just like any citizen preparing his income tax return; he'll take advantage of any legitimate opportunity to reduce his taxes before he signs his return.

Take this example: Over a period of two months a man sells a total of £150,000. If he is working under the schedule shown above, he would earn

£2,500 each month if his sales were equally divided over the period. If, however, he should so arrange his orders that in the first month he reported £35,000 and in the second £115,000, his total earnings would be £5,300 (£1,050 for sales of £35,000 and £4,250 for sales of £115,000). The shorter the reporting period the greater the opportunity to rig the system. I agree, £300 is not a fortune, but as ready money it will pay a few bills.

At first sight a regressive commission plan under which commission rates decline as sales increase doesn't make sense. I cannot conceive that a rational plan would lower a man's composite rate the more he sold. It is difficult to understand how a company can ethically reap the benefit of higher sales at the same time it increases its profits at the expense of the salesman.

The chart reproduced here illustrates the workings of a regressive plan. You will note it is the opposite of a progressive plan.

	Sales	*Commission rate*
Up to	£40,000	5%
From	£40,000 to £75,000	4%
Above	£75,000	3%

Thus, a man selling £40,000 would earn £2,000 (5 per cent of sales). If he sold £75,000, he would be paid £3,400 (4.67 per cent of sales), and on volume of £100,000 he would receive £4,150 (4.15 per cent of sales). Note in the last example that while his first £40,000 in sales paid him £2,000, the final £60,000 nets him only £2,150.

Yet, there are many advocates of a regressive system. Their first claim is that the system puts a brake on overselling and makes a man more willing to handle the other responsibilities of his job such as missionary work and service calls. There may be some validity to this approach, but what is management for? Can't it control its men? It might be wiser for a company to hire a good sales manager than deliberately to put a curb on sales. Goose and golden egg come to mind.

The advocates also say a regressive system tends to cause sales to flatten out, reducing the aberrations normally experienced. It would certainly be foolish for a salesman to lump his sales into a single pay period, but why use a sledge hammer to crack a nut? Management is the proper answer, not confiscation.

A third point is made that a regressive system is effective in industries where first orders are difficult to secure, but repeat orders are received almost automatically. In such a specialized industry it would seem more equitable to pay a substantial commission for an appropriate period of time on orders received from a new customer and a lower rate on reorders beyond that date.

Curiously, nowhere have I seen comments by advocates of a regressive rate plan on the reception given it by the individuals most concerned — the sales force. I should think a sales manager would have a difficult time explaining the rationale of it to his men.

The final and strongest argument advanced by proponents of a regressive system is that it prevents salesmen from earning too much money — so much they are reluctant to accept promotion, so much that they will make more than the sales manager and even higher company officials. We are told that the career-minded salesman's ultimate goal is advancement to loftier levels of responsibility. This is undoubtedly true for many men, but the most percipient and successful of them realize that promotion into management often occasions an exchange of income for prestige and authority.

Who ever said that the best salesman made the best manager? Only in exceptional cases is this a fact. The supersalesmen are often loners, many of them are selfish, thinking more of themselves than of their employers. They are reluctant to allow anything to interfere with their eternal quest for sales. They are disdainful of new men, not eager to waste time helping them. New men are the opposition that soon will be out in the field making sales that rightfully belong to them.

Many of the superstars exhibit traits directly opposed to those valued in a sales manager. This breed of salesmen can be egotistical and hard headed. They do not suffer fools gladly. Make such a man a sales manager and you lose a top producer and take the chance of destroying a whole sales organization. Where is it written in words of fire that a top salesman shouldn't earn more than his boss?

The more a man produces the more he should be paid because for every pound he makes the company makes several. Let the sales force sell everything it can sell as long as the factory can supply the goods. If it can't the sales force will find a new home. The higher the level of sales the more profit the company makes even with a progressive commission plan.

Once the basic target has been achieved, the incremental sales are the most profitable the company can make. Fixed costs being covered, the gravy becomes richer. A chart will serve to illustrate this point. Perhaps I have oversimplified the figures, but the basic principle of the incremental approach is sound.

The corporation budget projected sales of £700,000 for the year at a factory production cost of £500,000. It expects to incur selling expenses of £140,000. The margin thus becomes £60,000. Factory costs include materials and direct labour of £200,000 and fixed overhead of a like amount.

XYZ CORPORATION

	Projected results	*20 per cent increase in sales*
Material and labour	£200,000	£40,000
Fixed overhead	200,000	—
Variable overhead	100,000	20,000
Cost of goods sold	£500,000	£60,000
Sales	700,000	140,000
Gross margin	200,000	80,000
Selling expenses (20 per cent of sales)	140,000	28,000
Adjusted margin	£60,000	£52,000

This type of overhead remains the same no matter what level of production is achieved. It includes the cost of buildings and plant, the salaries of the plant manager, engineers, department heads and office workers. Once these costs are covered, they cease to be a charge against factory production costs.

Further overhead amounting to £100,000 is variable in nature. In other words, it is a function of the level of production in the factory. Cost of power to run machines longer and cost of additional supplies are examples of overhead costs that will rise when more goods are produced.

Let us assume that company products were well received by customers and the sales force did an excellent job, with the result that sales increased by 20 per cent over projections. Material and labour on the increase would cost £40,000 and variable overhead would cost an additional £20,000. The fact that there would be no further expense for fixed overhead would result in a gross margin for the additional sales of £80,000.

If selling expenses remained at a constant 20 per cent of sales, margin on the incremental sales of £140,000 would be £52,000 against a margin of £60,000 on the base sales £700,000. Even if selling expenses increased by 25 per cent on the incremental sales from £28,000 to £35,000 (a large increase even under a progressive commission rate), the additional margin of £45,000 would be 32 per cent of the incremental sales. On projected sales of £700,000 the margin of £60,000 is 8.6 per cent of sales.

If the regressive commission advocates held sway in XYZ Corporation, we could expect to see selling expenses on the incremental business reduced below £28,000 and the adjusted margin would increase by a like amount.

The economics of the situation lead me to favour doing whatever can be done to increase sales rather than making a strong effort to inhibit growth.

And I don't understand why the sales force should be denied the right to enjoy its share of the additional profits it helped the company to earn.

Now, I'll finish what I was saying about reward management of salesmen. No sales manager ever forgets the value of a great example. 'If Charlie can do it, so can you.' Salesmen profit from their own success, sales managers profit from the success of their men, and companies profit from the success of every employee.

Salesmen and sales managers are not clones and don't ever forget it. They operate on two different sets of values. It is quite possible that the best sales manager was never an outstanding salesman. Other attributes than the ability to sell in high volume make him a successful manager.

Years ago I had a top division manager, one of the finest men I ever knew. He was a great salesman, but he had the compassion and interest for his branch managers and salesmen that set him well apart from his peers. He had built a remarkably productive area of the country from absolutely nothing by his innate ability, personality and drive. His pay was based on the volume and profitability of his division.

One day the president of the company called me, saying he would be retiring soon and the board of directors had authorized him to offer the job to Obie, my division manager. The president, Paul, was polite enough to ask my permission before speaking to Obie. I told him to go ahead, but that Obie would turn him down, not revealing my reasons for the statement. Paul was highly indignant — who wouldn't give an eye tooth to be president? We bet a dinner at Brennans in New Orleans on the outcome.

Three days later Obie called me. 'The damndest thing happened,' he told me. 'Paul called me to New York and offered me the presidency of the company. How do you like that?' 'What did you tell him?' I asked. 'I turned him down,' Obie responded. 'Why?' Three reasons. One, I didn't think I'd like the work. Too many administrative duties, board meetings and all that. Two, I didn't think I was qualified to handle the job. I'm not a great intellect. All I know is people. Third, I didn't see why I should take a £100,000 cut in pay just to be president.'

Enough said on the subject except that Obie joined Paul and me in New Orleans and Paul picked up the tab for a superlative dinner.

Commission Based on Gross Margin

As time goes on, companies are giving ever greater attention to the profit margins of the products they sell. They are breaking away from the long-held conviction that increasing gross turnover is the ultimate sales objective. An important result of this shift in thinking is the growing trend toward giving weight to the relative profitability of products when establishing commission rates. To bring this about they introduce the gross margin concept. Simply stated, gross margin is sales price less cost of goods sold. A few figures will illustrate my point.

Product	*Gross margin*	*Sales*	*Margin*	*5 per cent commission*	*Net margin*
A	40%	£150,000	£60,000	£7,500	£52,500
B	20%	150,000	30,000	7,500	22,500

Product A carries twice the margin of Product B, yet a company paying commission on sales volume would reward salesmen equally no matter which product they sold. The margin, minus commission, of Product A is $2\frac{1}{3}$ times that of Product B.

If the company changed to the profitability concept as its basis of commission, it might pay 6 per cent commission on sales of Product A and 4 per cent on B. The Product A salesman would receive £9,000 commission and the other man would be paid £6,000. Reward would be more in line with the value of the sales to the corporation. The net margin on Product A, £51,000, would be more than twice the £24,000 net on Product B.

Companies paying commission on a gross margin basis should not lose sight of the importance of sales of high-volume products, even though they carry low margins. Overhead is spread over production costs and the sale of high-volume items contributes heavily to the absorption of fixed costs.

Two methods are employed to pay commission on the gross margin basis. The first is to list the margin of all products and provide each salesman with a copy. The overriding disadvantage of this method is that the salesmen are privy to information the company undoubtedly regards as confidential. Yet, salesmen would consider withholding this information from them unacceptable. Without it, how could they check the accuracy of their pay cheques?

The second method avoids this dilemma. The full line of products is divided into groups, depending on their gross margins. Commission rates would be highest for the most profitable category. Here is an example of what might be done.

Product group	*Gross margin*	*Commission rate*
A	Over 50%	4.5%
B	40–49%	4.0%
C	30–39%	3.5%
D	Below 30%	3.0%

The salesman is told the classification of each product and the applicable commission rate, enabling him to confirm the accuracy of his commission statement. His commission is, of course, based on gross sales volume rather than gross margin, but the effect of this method of payment is to reward the salesman for selling the more profitable items. He is not aware of the gross margin of individual products. All he knows is that a certain item is class A and when he sells it his commission rate is 4.5 per cent.

It would be incumbent on the company to review constantly the costs of all products and keep groupings up to date. Switches from one category to another would have to be announced immediately to the sales force.

There are many advantages to this method of paying commission regardless of the breadth of the lines offered by a company. No matter what method of payment is employed, it is essential that the salesmen have a clear and complete understanding of it.

Straight Commission Plans

From salesman's viewpoint	**From company's viewpoint**
FIXED COMMISSION RATE	
Incentive to increase production Easy to understand Few disputes	Encourages sales force to higher sales level Easy to administer Simple to explain
PROGRESSIVE RATE	
Even stronger incentive to sell Opportunity to schedule orders in pay periods advantageous to salesman	An effective tool in increasing sales Results in additional selling costs, which should be absorbed by higher sales volume Requires strong management to prevent abuses in: 1. Manipulating orders 2. Overselling

Straight Commission Plans *(continued)*

From salesman's viewpoint	From company's viewpoint
REGRESSIVE RATE	
Advocates claim it should encourage salesmen to get promoted out of selling and into management Note: In all fairness it must be stated that because of circumstances peculiar to them, some companies operate in an environment in which a regressive-rate system is superior to other methods of compensation. It will be the obligation of the sales manager to determine whether his company is a member of that group.	Advocates claim it: Reduces threat of overselling Makes men more amenable to handle job responsibilities other than selling Evens out peaks and valleys in sales More accurately rewards selling efforts when first sale is difficult to secure, but reorders are to great extent automatic Prevents salesman from earning too much money
GROSS MARGIN BASE	
Encourages salesmen to make more money by selling high-margin products Will please those who do sell this type of product; will displease those who don't Could result in closer relationship with company. Men are made aware of what sales are of greater benefit to the company. What benefits the company benefits them also.	Incentive to men to sell more profitable products benefits company Amount of commission paid by company is more closely related to value of sales to the company Reward more nearly approximates contribution

Hints to Sales Managers

- Check all commission plans before choosing one.
- Your prime responsibility is to your company, but don't forget your men rely on you to represent their interests firmly and fairly.
- Sometimes it does pay to spend a buck to make one, two or three.
- Remember your interests are basically the same as your sales force's. All of you are trying to succeed and it takes a mutual effort for everyone to achieve his or her goal.
- The more you do to relate contribution to reward the better is the job you do for your company and your sales team.

Chapter 5

MANUFACTURER'S REPRESENTATIVES, INDEPENDENT CONTRACTORS AND DISTRIBUTORS

Many companies find it economically infeasible to maintain a conventional sales force in all of their selling areas. Perhaps a section of territory is so large and sparsely populated that the expense of covering the widely scattered potential accounts would be exorbitant considering the sales that might be obtained. Yet, business is available in the area and would be profitable if an inexpensive method of coverage could be employed.

Other companies of limited resources might sell a narrow range of inexpensive products. To them an average order is small and a salesman would have to write an impossibly large number of tickets to make a living. His travelling expenses would be high and his earnings seriously limited. The business he might obtain would be profitable neither to him nor his employer. Once again, the sales are there; the problem is to secure them and at the same time make a profit.

In still another case, a company's sales might be highly seasonal by nature, with nearly all of its volume coming during a relatively short period of three or four months. Consider, for example, the monthly sales graph of a tennis racket manufacturer. A ski equipment manufacturer on the other hand, would have a sales drought lasting from April through October.

If we add to our pair of companies another that specializes in seeds and home garden tools and a fourth that concentrates on souvenirs for sale to tourists, we would cover a year during which there would be a steady demand for at least one group of the products we have described.

A conglomerate owning all four companies could operate successfully with its own sales force provided the men were resilient enough to shift selling gears every three or four months.

A salesman representing a single company would starve unless he could hibernate for at least two-thirds of the year. Even, then, unlike a bear, he would still have to pay the mortgage every month.

Yet, companies do have the means to earn welcome profits despite the conditions described above. They use manufacturer's representatives, independent contractors or distributors. The first two have much in common, the major difference being that in most cases an independent contractor sells the products of one company while the manufacturer's representative, as his name implies, sells for several companies.

Quite often independent contractors are fully or semi-retired former employees of a company who work a few hours a week to supplement retirement income. Manufacturer's reps, usually full-time salesmen, customarily handle noncompeting products of the companies they represent, supplying a varied line of items in demand by their customers. Some reps deal in raw materials or supplies used by industrial factories, others sell to retail establishments such as hardware stores. Still others might carry supply items for hotel or fast food chains. It would be unusual to find a manufacturer's rep who dealt with more than one type of consumer. In general, they sell only to customers of similar classification and requirements.

Manufacturer's reps and independent contractors are usually individuals who operate without the benefit of support personnel. Only in exceptional cases do they maintain an inventory of the merchandise they offer. When orders are secured they are forwarded to the corporation for filling. Invoicing can be made by either party. Reps are compensated for no expenses and are paid on a straight commission basis. They usually operate in clearly defined territories and are granted exclusive rights to all sales emanating from the area.

Distributors operate quite differently. Often they maintain fully equipped general offices, employ a number of salesmen and operate sizeable warehouses containing an inventory of commodity type products of the companies they represent. Like the manufacturer's reps, they receive no expense allowance and are paid either by commission or a system of discounts on the products they handle.

Independent contractors are exactly what the name implies. They are independent, sometimes excessively so. As they represent a single company, it is possible to exert a modicum of control over them, but by the nature of their business they are masters of their fate. One advantage they have over manufacturer's reps from the company point of view is that their efforts are not spread over the products of a number of companies. The one company they represent is assured that whatever effort they expend is expended for its benefit.

A few more words on manufacturer's reps and distributors, the major source of sales not obtained through company employees. The sales manager who controls, or more precisely, who attempts to control their activities is confronted by a number of problems, some administrative and others motivational.

Early on, he realizes that his independent agents do not have the loyalty he would expect from employee salesmen. His agents often serve many masters. Length of relationship might exert a positive influence, but fundamentally agents' hearts are in their pocketbooks and the lines most profitable to them command their greatest attention. Even if his line is the most valuable to an agent, the sales manager is not home free; if his products are in a less important category, his problems are multiplied.

The sales manager's primary objective is to make it as easy as possible for the agent to make money by selling his line in volume. To do this he must provide training in the use and application of his products and assist in developing selling techniques. No agent can sell successfully items he does not understand fully.

The agent is a busy man. His many masters impose a multitude of demands on him and it is not always easy for the sales manager to schedule enough time with a new rep to make him familiar with the manager's line and, once that is done, to keep him abreast of developments and changes in the line. Constant communication with the agent is essential, as are visits to him in the field.

The most frequent complaint voiced by sales managers is that agents do not spend enough time promoting their particular company's products. A legitimate complaint, it is true, but consider the plight of the agent. He represents a dozen clients and each demands 20 per cent of his time. This conflict illustrates the fundamental problem inherent in selling through independent agents.

Sales managers also feel that agents do not spend enough time developing new accounts. Again a justifiable concern, but in this respect are agents much different from company-employed salesmen?

Put it this way: basically a sales manager throws his products into a pot with many other noncompeting items. He hopes the agent will give him a square deal and attempts to encourage this by paying a generous commission, training the agent to the extent he will accept direction and keeping in as close touch with him as possible. The results obtained will depend on how successful the manager's efforts are and the quality of the man he has chosen to represent his company.

Despite the difficulties in operating with manufacturer's reps and distributors, this method of selling has advantages when it is uneconomic for a company to use its own salesmen in an area. The costs of selling by independent agents are entirely variable. No costs are incurred until a sale is made. The amount of commission is fixed and the company is not obligated to defray any selling expenses of the agent.

Thus, all sales made should be profitable. To secure them the sales manager assumes additional responsibilities and extra duties, but he is paid to do his job and it includes managing his independent agents.

Use of Manufacturer's Agents, Independent Contractors and Distributors

BENEFITS

Enables company to cover territories that will not support a salesman because:

1. Potential too low
2. Company products low in price and average sale small
3. Business too seasonal to support a salesman

All sales made should be profitable because:

1. Company's only obligation is to pay commission on sales
2. No other selling expenses are reimbursed

PROBLEMS ENCOUNTERED

Lack of control over activity of agents
They may have little loyalty to your company
A negative influence will be encountered if your products are merely an unimportant sideline to the agent
It is difficult:

1. To develop an aggressive sales attitude on the part of agents for your products
2. To instruct agents on products and selling techniques.
3. To spend time in field with them.
4. To encourage them to canvass for new accounts
5. To secure adequate selling time for your products
6. To select the most effective agent

Frequent communication with agents may be difficult to maintain
Heavy demands are placed on the time of the sales manager

Hints to Sales Managers

- Be selective in choice of agents.
- Investigate character and references thoroughly.
- Check other products handled.
- Check calibre and reputation of other companies represented.
- Will your line be a major component or relatively unimportant to the agent?
- Does the general line of products carried by the agent indicate he now sells to customers who are potential users of your products?
- Are there many potential users of your products in the area with which the agent has had little or no contact? If so, can he be relied on to generate business for you from them?

Once an arrangement for representation has been made:

- Do everything in your power to instruct the agent in the specifications and uses of your products
- Provide as much sales training as possible so your products will be presented to customers in the best light.
- Maintain constant communication with the agent.
- Spend time in the field with him, especially with the object of opening new accounts.
- Keep him abreast of new developments in your company — new products, sales techniques and so forth.

Chapter 6

ADVANCES, BONUSES, PROFIT SHARING, FRINGE BENEFITS

We've already talked about salary and commissions and digressed for a few minutes discussing reps and distributors. Now we'll return for further consideration of other reward schemes for salesmen.

Advances

The use of advances negates to a considerable extent the lack of security felt by persons paid on a straight-commission basis. A non-guaranteed draw is really nothing but an advance against earnings. Shortages not covered in lean months are recoverable from income in richer ones. Accounting is continual and overdrafts are never forgiven.

A guaranteed draw is similar to a minimum salary and failure to cover the draw is forgiven at the end of the accounting period, usually one year. Thus, a man who failed by £2,500 to cover his draw in the course of a calendar year would have the shortage written off and start the new year even with the board. Had he been on a non-guaranteed draw, the overdraft would continue to hang over his head until repaid.

Advances are effective in highly seasonal businesses in which salesman's earnings are concentrated in a few months and long arid spells are normal. They are also excellent for starting a new man in business. Some companies put a recruit on a guaranteed draw for a period of time, switch him to a non-guaranteed draw when he should be able to earn his keep and finally put him on the regular company reward scheme when his apprenticeship has been completed.

Salesmen would, of course, much prefer a straight salary to an advance as they learn a business. For that matter they would prefer a salary over an advance at any time. There are no strings attached to a salary. A salesman paid a combination of salary and commission keeps every penny he gets paid. Exchange the salary for a draw and it's a whole new ball game.

Other types of earnings such as commission, bonus or profit sharing are usually included in a reward scheme featuring a draw and the draw is charged against them before final settlement is made with a salesman. There is a feeling of permanence about a salary that is missing in a draw. Yet, it is easier to switch a man from either type of draw to commission than it is to take away his salary and require him to support himself from then on through his commission earnings alone.

As a matter of fact, companies that do shift from salary to commission plans experience a larger than normal turnover of salesmen. As might be expected, many of the men who leave are the lower producers who would suffer a severe drop in earnings as a result of the change. Advances against commissions focus a man's attention on the importance of selling to earn a livelihood.

Bonuses

The eye of every salesman lights up when he hears the magic word *bonus*. Paying a bonus is a method a company adopts to reward special contribution and as an incentive to superior performance. Surveys have indicated that more than half the companies paying bonuses pay them annually, one fourth pay quarterly and the balance is almost equally divided between semi-annual and periods under three months.

The annual period has much to recommend it. To earn his bonus the salesman must apply himself to the job for a whole year and there is less reason for him to manipulate sales than there would be were the bonus based on production over a shorter period. In seasonal industries or those with frequent peaks and valleys the longer period would appear to be preferable. A simple chart will illustrate this point.

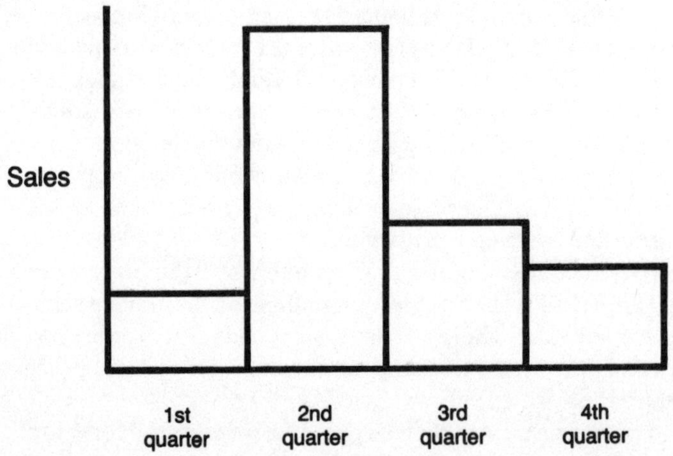

With a sales pattern similar to the one shown, a company that offered a standard quarterly bonus would pay through the nose in the second quarter and probably no salesman would reach bonus-earning production in any other period. The company should either base the bonus on sales for the entire year or establish different targets for each quarter. The purpose of a bonus is to reward a salesman for doing a good job for the company. Bonuses that are too easily earned do not benefit the company and those that are impossible to attain do no one any good.

Discretionary Bonus

A discretionary bonus is one declared out of company profits. The amount of the appropriation depends on the success of the company during the preceding year and is subject to the approval of company executives or the board of directors. There is an element of uncertainty about this type of bonus: the company may have just completed a profitable year, but the directors may be concerned about the coming one and decide a conservative policy, particularly with regard to cash, should be adopted. Thus the normal bonus appropriation may be cut. On the other hand, a company might despite less-than-satisfactory results last year, appropriate a substantial sum for bonuses if the future looks better.

The element of uncertainty is the principal weakness of a discretionary bonus. Since determination of interim profits is uncertain, most organizations that pay bonuses of this type use the entire fiscal year as a base, paying bonuses a month or two after the close of the year.

Once an amount has been set up in a bonus pool, it is necessary to distribute it as equitably as possible. Again the element of uncertainty is present. An example will illustrate this point.

Suppose a company appropriates the sum of £100,000 to be distributed to its sales force as a bonus. The country is divided into seven regions, each of which has several branches. The number of salesmen totals approximately 200.

How is the pot to be split? Good question. Does each region get one seventh of the bonus pool? That might be equitable provided all regions were of comparable size and performed equally well, but it's a sure bet they weren't and didn't. Should the money be allocated by branch in accord with ranking depending on percentage of target reached? A good approach, but what about the top salesman in the whole company? He was the only good producer in his branch, but despite his record performance the branch ranked well below average.

Should branch managers submit lists of worthy candidates for a bonus to regional managers who would send them along to the sales director at the home office who would make the final decision? If the sales director were a diligent and conscientious man and studied all the recommendations submitted to him, the lucky recipient of a bonus would be fortunate to receive his bonanza in time to celebrate Christmas.

All this should indicate it is not easy to distribute a discretionary bonus in a fair and timely fashion when a large number of salesmen are involved. A company with only ten or twenty salesmen finds the solution simpler. A much more accurate distribution can be made, but other problems replace the ones that have been avoided.

Do old school ties influence the distribution? How important is age, sex, or years of service in determining the amount of an award? When a subjective judgement is made, a charge of favouritism is never far behind. The unfortunate result is that even though the allocation was made with the judgement of a Solomon it will not be so perceived by a large segment of the sales force. When bad feelings are created, the effect on an organization is immediately apparent. Morale drops and so do sales.

Should the sales manager decide to divide the bonus allocation of his branch equally among his men he will fare no better. The higher producers will scream that they have been robbed while the new and weaker salesmen will applaud his wisdom.

Unless discretionary bonuses are distributed under an accurate, fair and clearly understood plan they can do as much harm as good. The secret is to develop criteria on which to base the award. We'll go into this more deeply when we summarize our conclusions on bonuses.

Fixed Bonus

The other type of bonus can be described as fixed. It is regarded as an extra reward for special performance and can be built into each salesman's reward agreement. Targets are often used to determine fixed bonus awards.

A graded scale of bonus credits might be given for meeting or exceeding targets. Bonus might start at 90 per cent of target, paying a modest amount for reaching that figure. For each 5 per cent sold above that level the bonus would be figured at rates that would increase as each new plateau was achieved. An example of how such a plan might work is shown below.

I should make it clear that the figures in this and other charts appearing throughout this book are not offered as recommendations for your use in setting up a reward scheme. The purpose of the chart is to outline a method of developing a plan to meet the needs of your company. The figures are for illustrative purposes only.

The bonus might also be figured based on a salesman's gross earnings. Each year when the sales manager reviewed with a salesman his target, his projected earnings for the period would have been figured. The salesman would earn a bonus for reaching 90 per cent of that figure and each

Salesman A — Target £250,000

Bonus for reaching	90 per cent of Target	=	¼ per cent of sales
Bonus for reaching	95 per cent of Target	=	½ per cent of sales
Bonus for reaching	100 per cent of Target	=	¾ per cent of sales
Bonus for reaching	105 per cent of Target	=	1 per cent of sales

(Continue as far as you like)

increment above that would be rewarded, the amount increasing as each level of earnings was reached.

Let us assume salesman A in the example was expected to make £25,000 if he met his target of £250,000. His bonus plan could be set up this way:

Salesman A — Projected earnings £25,000

Bonus when earnings reach	£22,500	£ 500
Bonus when earnings reach	£23,750	700
Bonus when earnings reach	£25,000	1,100
Bonus when earnings reach	£26,250	1,500

(Continue as far as you like)

The plans differ in one respect only: one bonus depends on achievement relative to sales target and the other on achievement relative to total earnings. It would appear that whichever approach was taken would matter little, but further analysis discloses a fallacy in this thinking. Consider one salesman paid on a straight commission earning £25,000 and another earning a like amount who receives half his compensation through salary.

We would identify the major responsibility of the first man as generating sales and either bonus plan would suit him equally well. What about the other chap? Many of his activities are focused in other areas than selling and because of that he has a comparatively low sales target. To base his bonus solely on sales would be a mistake.

He might earn a large bonus if he neglected his other duties and conentrated on sales. On the other hand, his sales production might be little better than adequate, but he could make extremely valuable contributions in discharging his non-selling obligations. He would receive no bonus unless a method of assessing his total effort were designed.

If criteria other than sales are important in determining the value of a man's contribution, the bonus might be divided into two portions. The first would depend on sales production and the second on the man's performance of the other responsibilities of his job: missionary calls, opening new accounts, training new men, service work and so forth.

The bonus allocated to sales would be based on his target and the formula used to compute it should be thoroughly understood by the man. The other part of the bonus would perforce depend partly on quantifiable activities, such as opening accounts and training new men, and partly on the best subjective judgement of the sales manager when there is no way to measure performance mathematically.

It should be the aim of management to remove, as much as possible, subjective judgements in determining the amount of a bonus. The more uncertainty that can be taken out of a bonus policy the better for everyone involved.

We are told that two-thirds of companies base bonuses on attainment of targets, either turnover or gross margin. The remainder use new accounts, reduction in selling expenses, management conception of value of contribution made, group performance or other criteria to control distribution. In some cases a combination of criteria determine the amount of bonus to be paid.

Office Bonus

It is not unusual for a branch or a district to win a company bonus for meeting or exceeding its target. Ordinarily such sums are relatively modest in amount and the sales manager may distribute the bonus at his discretion. He might throw a banquet for his whole organization, use the money as a prize fund or distribute a portion of it to men who had done a special service in the past year for which they received no direct reward. He might even decide to reward members of the office staff who had been instrumental in the success of the organization.

General Discussion on Bonuses

A word of caution. Fixed bonuses are paid irrespective of the performance of the company. Company sales and profits may be down, but a handful of talented salesmen will probably sail by their targets and earn substantial bonuses. These payments will increase selling expenses to an extent determined by the number of men who do exceed their targets. Perhaps this might be considered unfortunate from the company point of view, but the cost is minimal compared with the even worse results if no salesman sold enough to earn a bonus.

Of a more serious nature are the problems encountered when a company deliberately keeps salesmen's salaries and commissions low and customarily pays a substantial discretionary bonus to bring earnings to projected levels. All salaries are a fixed expense and companies attempt to keep them to a minimum on the theory that it should seldom if ever be necessary to cut them in bad times. From the point of view of the company this approach has many advantages, but how does the salesman react when his year-end bonus is cut in half because the company has suffered a disappointing year?

Salesman unconsciously consider the customary bonus to be an integral part of disposable income, as fixed as their salary. They go into debt during the year and let bills pile up knowing that all will be well when bonuses are received. The reduced payment leads to financial disaster and emotional trauma.

The executive or the committee that distributes discretionary bonuses is always subject to charges of prejudice and favouritism. It is not unknown that at times the charges may be well founded. It is difficult if not impossible to devise a method of payment that rewards each person in an administrative position equitably and accurately. Personal judgement must be relied on, but when nearly absolute measures of performance are available as in the case of salesmen it makes sense to use them.

Profit Sharing

Many experts in the field of sales management disapprove of the payment of profit sharing to salesmen. For once I agree with them. There may be an argument in favour of such a payment if no bonus plan is established for excellence in sales performance. When an adequate plan is or can be put into effect, however, profit sharing is redundant.

Who can determine the precise source of additional or unusual company profit? Sales were up, probably, but why were they up? Extra hard work on the part of the sales force? Possibly, but equally possibly the rise might be attributed to substantial cost savings in manufacturing that enabled the company to hold or even reduce price levels. Research may have developed a product superior to anything offered by the competition. The board of directors might even have lopped a few million off the payroll by getting rid of dead wood at the home office.

If management wishes to reward the men and women who brought about the higher profit, let it discover what and who was responsible and reward the deserving individual or group. Salesmen will derive their benefit from improved products they sell at more competitive prices.

At times corporate accounting is so sophisticated that regional, division and even branch profits can be determined accurately. When dependable profit information is available it would be unusual if a regional manager did not have a profit-sharing clause in his contract and the same could be said for division managers. Often the melon is cut carefully enough that a slice is made available to branch managers who stand high on the profit list.

This practice I applaud. If an outstanding job is done, the individuals responsible should be rewarded. Profit sharing paid to a branch manager is different from a bonus given a branch office. If a branch is profitable the credit should go to its manager, and to reward him for the success of his efforts is fitting and proper.

What happens when one or two branches or even divisions are highly profitable even though overall the company suffers near disaster in a year? The ability of the company to pay cannot be ignored and if profit sharing were payable on a discretionary basis the men involved might receive little or nothing for their efforts.

On the other hand, had a policy been adopted under which all managers — regional, division or branch — received a fixed percentage of the profit made in their offices they would be paid irrespective of the condition of the company.

Profit sharing, like bonuses, can be either discretionary or fixed. Choosing one method or the other can cause complications for each of the parties involved.

Fringe Benefits

Fringe benefits have become a fascinating subject and an item of considerable expense to a corporation. The costs of fringes vary to as high as 40 per cent of direct compensation expense, depending on what benefits are offered and whether a portion of the expense is shared with the employee.

Historically, salesmen were the last group to participate in the fringes made available by companies to their employees. Salesmen were reluctant to change their long-established reputation as mavericks. Surveys made in the 1950s and 1960s disclosed that they preferred more generous commission rates to the fringes offered to others by their companies. However, times have changed and at present nearly all full-time salesmen enjoy the benefits available to other employees.

Every employer and employee is required to pay National Insurance, as well as Income Tax on earnings. From that point on there are any number of benefits a company can offer its employees. Among them are: pension plans, health and hospital insurance, life and accident insurance, membership in civic or professional associations, contribution for children's education, matching funds for gifts to charitable or educational institutions, and almost everything else you can think of. Not least, of course, is the company car; not just a tool of the of the saleman's trade but a status symbol — which may these days just as easily be a BMW as a Ford. But 'car policy' is a complex and emotive, issue; one that would justify a book in its own right.

No performance qualification is required for eligibility for a fringe benefit although it is usual to establish a waiting period before a new employee is entitled to certain benefits. Some companies absorb the entire cost of such benefits as life and accident insurance while others require the employee to pay part of the cost.

Many companies feel that fringe benefits they provide must be in line with those offered by the competition. I would imagine that few salesmen would seek a job with a particular company only because of the value of the fringes it offered, but a salesman might be reluctant to join a company if he had to pay the major portion of the cost of the few benefits made available to him. He might decide a company niggardly with benefits might also be reluctant to reward good sales production adequately.

Fringe benefits are now a fact of life for all employers. Those expenses are escalating and there appears to be little evidence that the future will see any reduction in either benefits or their cost.

Other Methods of Reward

From salesmen's viewpoint	From company's viewpoint
ADVANCES	
Prefer guaranteed to non-guaranteed Much prefer salary If salary not offered, salesmen, especially new and weaker men, welcome draw for the steady income it provides	Good if business is highly seasonal Effective when used to reward men getting started in business
BONUSES	
Prefer fixed bonus Too much uncertainty, with discretionary type and suspicion about method of distribution	Discretionary 1. Problems arise in allocation 2. Can lead to lower morale 3. Controllable expense Fixed 1. Excellent incentive when properly based 2. Cost will be determined by sales performance. Projections should be included in expense budget

Other Methods of Reward *(continued)*

From salesman's viewpoint	From company's viewpoint
BONUS—OFFICE	
	Good for morale of office staff if wisely used. For best results should be based on overall performance of organization
PROFIT SHARING	
Poor substitute for fixed-bonus plan Unreliable in amount and controlled by overall company profits	As part of reward scheme for salesmen, inferior to bonus as motivator Good to reward all levels of sales management when accounting system can determine office profits accurately
FRINGES	
Generally approve any benefits not too expensive to them Good benefits may aid in improving salesmen's perception of company	Benefits should be competitive with those of others in industry Must be concerned with total costs of benefits Benefits are a tool for improving morale of salesmen and building loyalty

Hints to Sales Managers

- Compare advances of both types before choosing one, and also compare effectiveness and cost of such advances with salary.
- In setting up a bonus plan, avoid as far as possible the necessity to make subjective judgements.
- Rely on hard data—sales production, new accounts opened, new men trained.
- But if a salesman's value to the company also depends on qualitative factors, consider them impartially and equitably.
- Don't forget to include the estimated cost of bonuses in your budget for sales expenses.
- Encourage top management to institute a profit-sharing plan for your office, division or region. It will cost the company, but the return from it should be substantially greater than the expense incurred.
- Analyse competitors' fringe-benefits packages before preparing your own.

Chapter 7

PRIZE CONTESTS

Though a number of salesmen year after year win valuable prizes offered by their employers, it is not proper to consider awards as an ingredient of a total reward package. This is so even though the tax people require that the value of most prizes be included in a salesman's earnings. Prizes should be considered as an additional fringe benefit, a perk that a salesman can secure by superior performance. No responsible sales manager would consider including the value of prize expected to be won in setting a target earnings figure for one of his men.

We are including this chapter in the book because prizes can, like some forms of true compensation, provide strong incentives to salesmen to increase their earnings through extra effort. When well-planned, prize contests, like bonuses, assist companies and the men who represent them to attain their goals. Thus it is appropriate for us to consider the theory and practice of offering contests to salesmen.

Prize contests are used by a company to stimulate additional sales effort by its men or to direct attention toward specific short-term company goals. They can be remarkably effective if designed and handled properly or highly damaging if planning is faulty.

Contests are a fact of life for companies and we'll spend a few pages on the theory underlying their use as well as comment on the design and promotion of effective contests.

A company can have several reasons for offering a contest to its men:

1. To increase volume of gross sales. This might be a long-term objective
   of a company and the contest would also be long-term in nature — at least three months and perhaps a year.
2. To push special products or over-stocked items. Such a goal would be short-term and the contest would also be a short one. Care would have to be taken to avoid preoccupation with the contest detracting excessively from overall sales objectives.
3. To open new accounts. Such a contest ordinarily would be of short duration.

In general, contests based on important long-range objectives will last longer than those directed at less vital short-term goals. The value of the prizes offered varies with the relative importance of the desired objective. It is not feasible to adjust reward schemes frequently enough to achieve relatively minor goals and contests are effective means to attain results without disturbing overall policies.

Not every corporation approves of or uses contests to stimulate its men. They have basic objections to the practice and many are, to an extent, valid.

Contests are habit forming. Once addicted, withdrawal is difficult. This argument is valid only if the contests are not productive to the company. If they are, why should they be stopped? The men enjoy and profit from stimulating contests and the company also profits. What more could anyone ask?

Development and promotion of a good contest is time consuming. I agree. So is everything a sales manager does. Anything that helps a company and the sales force is part of the job he is paid to do.

Contests based on gross sales volume can cause overselling and slumps before and after the contest. This is certainly true in many industries. For example, a salesmen selling raw steel to a dozen customers has little opportunity to increase his overall production. Manufacturing schedules at factories require just so many tons of steel a month. An increase in orders one month will be deducted from the next month's shipment.

The same argument does not hold true, however, for what I call 'creative selling'. A house-to-house salesman selling vacuum cleaners may sell one machine for every four demonstrations he makes. More demonstrations means more sales and there is no limit to the number of doorbells he can push. There must be several million men and women engaged in similar types of selling and the extra effort engendered by a contest puts more money into their pockets and the company coffers.

Another complaint asks why should a company pay a man twice for doing the same job? The operative word here is 'same'. If a contest programme is properly set up the salesman won't be doing the same job; he will do better than usual and the prize is an extra reward for extra performance. Prizes should be paid like bonuses — on the basis of achievement.

Another objection to contests cites the negative effect on individuals and groups of salesmen who do not win or who know they cannot win as soon as they learn the requirements for winning. The culprit here is not contests in general, but how that particular one was designed. Prizes offered to one or two top producers will be of no interest to the rest of a sales force. If a contest requires a single sale for a man to qualify for a prize and it is awarded by the random selection of one of a hundred entrants, the contest will fail. All contests shouldn't be given a bad rap because a few are poorly set up.

The charge is made that contests are childish, beneath the dignity of mature men and women. Have you ever seen a £50,000 a year salesman agonizing over a ten-foot side hill putt on the 18th green with £2 riding on the outcome? I'm all in favour of it.

We've talked enough about poorly organized contests and what they won't do; let's take a look at the other side of the coin. In my opinion a well-designed and well-promoted sales contest can be a very strong influence in turning an average salesman into a star performer. Few salesmen, especially young and inexperienced ones, have any real conception of what they are capable of achieving. Some men don't seem to care, being content to crawl along in the comfortable rut. But one out of three or five is ready to explode if something lights his fuse. This is just what a contest can do.

Consider this situation. A company runs a three month contest and salesmen who sell 75 units in the period are offered their choice among several prizes. A relatively new man has sold 17 units in his best month. Among the prizes offered is a hi-fi system he would give his eye teeth to have, so he buckles down to work and sets out to win it. To his delight he sells 78 units and the hi-fi is his. The prize is important to him, but he has won something infinitely more valuable — knowledge that he is an excellent salesman and confidence in his ability to meet challenges he sets for himself. He worked hard for three months, of course, but now he knows he has the strength to achieve whatever he sets out to accomplish.

The most important benefit of a contest is the effect it can have on a large element of a sales force. Our friend has come close to doubling his earnings in the three-month period and the company has reaped a rich harvest of sales. If salesmen are stimulated, the company is bound to profit.

Many of the authorities seem to miss this point entirely. They can see only a temporary spurt in sales that will be reversed in the next month and ignore the lasting residual effect the contest might have on the lives of a number of its salesmen.

And don't ignore the value of a good example. Other men might not have quite the ability and drive of the man in our example, but an alert sales manager can capitalize on his success to motivate other men to follow in his footsteps.

Not long ago, a young woman I know decided to enter a marathon. She had been jogging for some time, but had never run as many as 10 miles. Her goal was to finish the 26 mile, 385 yard course and she was determined to do so. I don't know what her doctor would say about the project and I never asked her how long it took her to finish, but finish she did. She'll never run another marathon, that's for sure, but she told me that never again in her life would she doubt her ability to face and conquer any challenge she meets. She tested herself to the sticking point and came out on top.

One of the Greek philosophers said, 'Know thyself'. He had it right — we never know what we can accomplish until at some point we test ourselves to the utmost. When we do, the result can surprise us. A contest will be a good one if it appeals to the imagination of men and stimulates them to attempt something they never before believed possible.

In describing the major benefit of an effective contest I have referred only to its impact on the sales force and said nothing of what it can mean to a company. I don't have to. If a sales force is stimulated to superior performance, the company can't help but profit in like measure. Don't lose sight of that aspect of contests.

Planning a Major Contest

Let us assume that a company finds its sales volume running behind projections and decides to run a three-month contest expecting to get back on target. For the sake of simplicity we'll also assume the company sells a single major product so the contest will be based on unit sales. For other companies it could, just as easily, be based on total turnover of sales.

The first requirement will be to establish a contest cost budget based on the estimated incremental sales the contest will generate. Next a schedule will be made outlining the targets for winning the various categories of prizes. To it will be added an estimate of the number of winners, the total units they are expected to sell and the cost of the prizes to be awarded in each group.

The schedule might look like this:

Prize category	*Number of units to win*	*Number of winners*	*Units sold*	*Cost of prizes*	*Total cost*
A	30	160	4,800	£30	£4,800
B	45	110	4,950	60	6,600
C	60	60	3,600	100	6,000
D	75	15	1,125	200	3,000
Grand prizes		2	220	6,000	12,000
Total		347	14,695		£32,400
Cost per unit sold — £2.20					

So far so good, but now we've got to massage the figures around a bit. First, the cost of £2.20 per unit is a misleading figure. Without the contest, a predictable number of the product would be sold in the normal course of business. The contest cost should be applied against only the incremental sales it generates. The contest planner will check his estimates of units to be sold during the contest, subtract normally expected sales and come up with the extra sales the contest should produce. If the contest costs are spread over these sales and the expense per unit is within the contest budget all is well, if not, cost of prizes must be cut or qualification for winning raised.

In making these estimates the planner will not overlook two important factors. All salesmen will not win a prize, we can be certain of that, but many of the non-winners will make a valiant effort. Though they fail to reach the minimum number of 30 units they will sell substantially more than they would have had there been no contest.

In addition, a salesman who sells his 30th unit early in the third month does not take a three-week vacation; he shoots for the next category of prize, especially if one of the offerings is something he really wants to win. Perhaps he doesn't reach the magic number of 45, but he does sell 39. His extra earnings are welcome solace for missing his goal. Successful contests will generate sales in a variety of ways.

The company's financial officer might well blow his top when he learns that expensive trips are to be given to the top two salesmen in the contest. If they sell 100 units each, the cost will be £60 a unit. Pure madness. By his lights he's right, but the sales manager thinks differently. He knows the value of example, how the success of two men might fire the imagination of a number of others. He also knows that any big contest needs one or more equally impressive winners to drive home the message.

What if the cost of the contest goes well above budget? The company will be delighted since the contest will have generated more sales than anticipated. However, should trips be awarded to all men who sold a specified number of units, 100 for example, a serious problem could result if 20 men met the requirement, against an estimate of 2. The lesson to be learned here is that when the units sold can bear the cost of prizes awarded, the more the merrier, but when the cost of the prize far exceeds the contribution of the units sold to win it, care should be exercised to limit total liablity.

Should contest costs fall well short of budget, there could be two major causes: either the contest was poorly designed and promoted or winning requirements were set too high.

Types of Prizes

Prizes come in the form of cash, merchandise or travel. Offering cash prizes had several disadvantages. Primarily, there is no discount when buying cash. The cost of £100 is £100. Merchandise can be purchased at discounts ranging up to 50 per cent. There is more glamour attached to a £400 watch than to £200 in cash. Furthermore, cash is soon spent and forgotten while a watch can be a life-long reminder of achievement.

Trips are gaining in popularity as prizes, especially when they offer vacations at luxurious resorts or in foreign countries. A fully paid week-long trip to Paris, for a couple, with a room at the Ritz or the Crillon and a chauffeur-driven car at their disposal is enough to turn the head of even the most blasé salesman.

A variety of prizes should be available in each category. No one item will appeal to everyone and an attempt should be made to cater to as many tastes as possible. Home furnishings or appliances, recreational equipment or tools for hobbyists might be offered, whatever might appeal to a segment of the sales force.

Qualifications to Win

A contest with only one winner is bad enough, one in which nobody wins is worse. If a prize is awarded to every man, its value, and it can't be great, is cheapened. The best contests are those that provide an opportunity for everyone to participate with a reasonable chance of winning. That is why four categories of prizes plus the two grand prizes were offered in the example. A goal is set for all types of salesmen: low, medium and high producers. The first level of prizes should be within the reach of every man and incentive should increase as each plateau is reached.

You will note that in this contest competition among men is restricted to the race for the two top prizes. In every other case a salesman competes only with himself. The half dozen men at the top can handle rivalry. The losers will lick their wounds and resolve to do better next time. For the present they select the prize they did win and console themselves by figuring how much extra reward they earned during the contest.

Planning a Minor Group Contest

Assume the company wants to close out a product at a discount. The sales manager decides to run a two-week contest to take care of the situation. He must keep in perspective the relative unimportance of the project and not divert the entire attention of his men to this minor undertaking away from their main responsibilities. He divides his sales force into two groups of more or less equal talent. The contest announcement states that at its conclusion a dinner will be held — the winners to eat steak, the losers spaghetti.

Corny and childish, maybe, but a capable sales manager with a light touch can get plenty of mileage out of the contest and the men will enjoy it, too.

Promotion of a Major Contest

Such a programme is not to be entered into lightly or without meticulous preparation. It is customary to announce major contests at regional meetings with all sales people and their spouses as well as sales managers in attendance. The presence of spouses is important. They can be and usually are a potent motivational force.

Colour brochures containing photographs of all prizes are handed out. These will be useful to salesmen for contest closes. A separate sheet listing requirements to win in each group will also be distributed. Of course, samples of each prize will be unveiled at the gathering.

If possible, a five-minute colour movie showing the marvels of Paris, London or Rome will be run. Airlines and travel agencies make such films available.

Any experienced sales manager knows how to run a meeting of this type: calling on strong producers to pick the prizes they intend to win, asking for a few words from the spouse of a trip winner last year, getting pledges from all levels of salesmen. Note that not one word is said about more sales for the company. The emphasis is on increased earnings for the sales force plus the opportunity to win the prize of their choice.

Promotion of the contest continues until the last day. The company house organ lists regional leaders and makes much of the performance of new men. Personal notes, perhaps only a dozen words in all, flow to the men from all tiers of management. The sales manager spends evenings on the telephone encouraging his contestants. Short weekly branch meetings keep the pot boiling.

At the conclusion of the contest another regional meeting is held for winners and non-winners alike. The successful men receive their prizes and praise for their achievements; those who didn't win resolve to do better next time.

National Sales Conventions

Many companies hold annual meetings of their sales forces at well-known resorts. Opulent is the descriptive word. For four or five days, couples live in the lap of luxury, cosseted and catered to as if they were royalty. And royalty they are, for they earned the right to be there. Salesmen must qualify by meeting a production standard during the period since the last national convention or perhaps for a shorter period. Even branch sales managers are often required to earn the trip — a valuable prize. No couple winning it could bear the thought of not returning the following year.

If the contest for invitation lasts an entire year, new men and others, due to illness or other causes, will find themselves unable to meet the target. The company is prepared for this eventuality. At intervals it establishes new targets for the balance of the year to the point it may set a stiff requirement for the final month. Even a new man only a few months with the company can earn the right to attend, and that is fitting and proper. The prize is always there, ready to be won until the last possible moment.

Exploitation, critics shout, bribery and constant pressure to produce. Not a bit of it. In the first place, if he has a mind to, a salesman can turn a deaf ear to what is said about the contest and ignore the bulletins issued on it. Few will.

Exploitation is a popular word and it has a very explicit meaning. It is defined as the unjust or improper use of another individual for one's own profit. How far this is from the present situation. Salesmen are encouraged to increase their earnings and they are promised a valuable and attractive bonus if they succeed in doing so — the very opposite of exploitation.

If the salesman does increase his earnings, of course the company profits, but it doesn't make an extra penny until the salesman receives a reward for his effort. What could be more fair? It is entirely proper for a company to stimulate and supply incentive to its men for their own advantage.

Summary

The underlying purpose behind all the preparation and promotion of a contest is to make the salesman realize he has the ability and the opportunity to break the mental barriers he has set for himself, realize he is capable of functioning far more effectively than he ever has in the past. Perhaps he didn't win even the lowest category prize; yet if the contest was well enough designed that it fired his imagination, he very possibly averaged eight or nine units a month against his previous average of six. No prize, but a 30 per cent increase in earnings isn't a bad first step. Next time he will start from a higher level, his horizons will be broadened and his improvement can be even more dramatic when the realization sinks in that he has the power to accomplish whatever goal he sets for himself.

A contest can supply stimulation and offer incentive, but the salesman is the only one who can motivate himself. Few people, salesmen or, for that matter, anyone at all, ever function even close to their full potential. They have no concept of what they can accomplish if they make a conscientious and intelligent effort. It isn't easy to jar a person off dead centre. A contest that appeals to a man might supply the shove that starts him moving in the right direction.

People aspire to better themselves and salesmen are in a preferred position to do so. A sales manager who opens the eyes of his men to the opportunities awaiting them has given them a precious gift.

The company that regards a contest from the viewpoint of the additional sales it will produce during the weeks or months it runs misses its major value. The residual effect if a mere handful of men find they can maintain a higher level of productivity can last for years. And, think of the men who benefit themselves and their families by the new awareness of their capability.

Contests

From salesman's viewpoint	From company's viewpoint
Provide an opportunity to win a prize they would like to have.	If well planned and promoted will provide strong stimulation to sales force
Provide motivation to increase earnings	Will be successful only if they appeal to wide segment of sales force
Provide useful selling tool — the contest close	The cost can be controlled. The higher the cost of a well-designed plan, the more successful the contest. Additional costs are welcome if actual sales exceed projections
If requirements to win too high or prizes not worthwhile, salesmen will not be motivated	Unsuccessful contests damage morale, demotivate men
Salesmen like to be winners, to receive praise for accomplishment	Anything that increases a salesman's production and earnings benefits the company
Top producers will go all out to win the top prize	Consider the possible disadvantages of a contest before you decide on it.
All men will enjoy the give and take of a well-run minor contest	

Hints to Sales Managers

- Be realistic when planning a contest. Don't give away all the profit, but don't set requirements for winning so high that no one wins. The sales force will be turned off rather than on.
- Make it possible for every salesman to have the opportunity to win if he gives the contest his best shot.
- The wider the appeal of a contest the more successful will it be.
- Your primary target is the minds and imagination of your sales force. If they are fully motivated and have confidence in their ability to succeed, they will succeed.
- A good contest results in two major benefits: the salesmen are better off and so is the company. One cannot gain without the other being equally successful.
- Running a contest is hard work. Be ready for it.

Chapter 8

REWARD SCHEMES

A majority of reward schemes for sales people combine two or more of the payment methods we have discussed. The most widely used combinations are:

1. Salary plus commission
2. Salary plus bonus
3. Commission plus bonus
4. Salary plus commission plus bonus

Many more variations are possible if we substitute advances, either guaranteed or non guaranteed, for salary. And, don't forget incentive prizes as a source of income for a salesman or the value of fringe benefits paid by the employer.

The purpose of a combination scheme is to eliminate the weaknesses of individual components and at the same time retain their strengths. The salary element is usually most popular in old, well-established companies that enjoy stable sales. Other companies employing salary as the major element in compensation are those that place heavy emphasis on missionary work, service and other functions not directly connected with sales volume.

More weight is put on the commission component by growing companies concentrating on expanding their business. There, greater incentive is needed and generous commission rates will do much to assure top performance of salesmen.

There has been a recent trend by companies to emphasize incentive over salary. Salaries are escalating in our present economy and employers are becoming increasingly concerned with the rise in fixed costs. On the other hand, there are indications that salesmen, looking for security and stability of income, would welcome a plan that paid half of their income in salary.

When commission is less than 25 per cent of total earnings, its incentive effect is vitiated. The reward must be worth the effort or the salesman will not exert himself to achieve his selling potential.

The salary/commission combination is extremely popular, especially when earnings are divided nearly equally between the two. The salesman has the benefit of security and the company can offer a strong incentive to the salesman to do his best. In addition, if salary is an important part of the reward package, the company can exert considerable control over the salesman.

If advances, of either type, are used to 'replace' the benefits of salary, a subtle psychological change takes place. The salesman is grateful for the assured income, yet he does realize that it is nothing but an advance on the commissions he will earn. He appreciates the loan, but he would prefer a salary he could truly call his own. On the other hand, commission rates are lower if a saleman is receiving a salary, higher if he receives a draw that will be charged against commissions earned. Thus, the outstandingly productive salesman who has no problem covering his draw prefers the higher commission rates paid him under such a plan.

Whether a draw or a salary is to be paid is a decision each company should analyse before making a choice. The majority of companies use salary instead of advances when paying fixed rewards to salesmen.

Up to now we have been talking about salary, commission and advances. Let us see how four equally productive salesmen would make out under various reward schemes. We will assume each man has a sales target of £250,000, which he meets exactly, and an earnings target of £25,000.

Salesman	*Pay plan*	*Salary*	*Commission*	*Draw*	*Total earnings*
A	Salary	£25,000			£25,000
B	10 per cent commission		£25,000		25,000
C	£12,500 salary plus 5 per cent commission	12,500	12,500		25,000
D	Draw against 10 per cent commission		25,000		
		Draw	18,000		
			£7,000	£18,000	£25,000

It would make no difference financially which method of payment was adopted, either from the salesman's viewpoint or the company's. We could close our discussion right here if all salesmen could be relied on to do exactly what was expected of them, but that will never happen.

Let us suppose each man exceeded his sales target by 10 per cent, £25,000, or fell short of it by a like amount. How would his earnings be affected?

Salesman	10 per cent above target	10 per cent below target
A	—	—
B	£2,500	£(2,500)
C	1,250	(1,250)
D	2,500	(2,500)

What do we learn from these charts? Let's take the salesman's approach first. The salaried man receives the same pay whether he sells £225,000, £250,000 or £275,000. If his sales have dropped, he worries about a cut in salary next year; if they have increased, he marshals his arguments for asking for a pay rise. Whether his pay is raised or lowered, he is reasonably certain the adjustment, if it is in fact made, will not fully reflect the value of his overage or shortage in sales.

The commission man, B, is pleased when his sales rise; his earnings increase in direct proportion to his production. When the balance tips in the other direction he wonders if he wouldn't have been better off to take half his earnings in salary. His commission rate would be cut to 5 per cent, but when times were bad it would cost him only half of what he lost by remaining on straight commission.

Salesman C, whose earnings are based equally on salary and commission, has the same feelings, but in reverse order. When he sells well above target he wishes he were on straight commission: when business turns down he is pleased that his stable salary buffers the impact of the loss of commission.

Salesman D, the man supported by advances, has sentiments akin to those of B, the commission man. Whether he is on a guaranteed or non-guaranteed draw will concern him only if his commission earnings fall below his £18,000 draw. If he is on a guaranteed draw, he will not be required to repay the overdraft incurred in a bad year; if his draw is non-guaranteed, the shortage will be recovered from his earnings when they exceed the base of £18,000. His income, like that of salesman B, the commission man, fluctuates in direct relation to the fluctuation of his sales. He does not have the modifying effect of salary to smooth out his earnings.

The company's first concern might be financial — the impact on costs when sales rise or fall. The fixed nature of salaries might be of sizeable concern if a drop in sales is deep and prolonged. On the other hand, the increase in commission costs when sales rise should not disturb the company since the added expense would be covered by the income generated by the incremental sales.

I should think the company would be interested in much more than the purely monetary aspects of the rise or fall in the compensation of its sales force that accompanied similar gyrations in sales. It would question the effectiveness of its reward. Had it been formulated wisely? Was it assisting the company to reach its sales objectives? Were the salesmen adequately and equitably paid? Finally, were the salesmen given the incentive necessary for them to fulfil all the responsibilities of their jobs?

In short, salesmen are concerned primarily with income and security, while the company must take a broader view of the effectiveness of its reward scheme.

When the bonus ingredient is added to a reward pot, the mixture emits a heady aroma, the faintest whiff of which makes a salesman's mouth water. The best salesmen are endowed with a strong competitive spirit; set a goal for them and they'll strive to reach it. Offer a valuable prize for success and they will redouble their efforts. Bonuses provide a powerful stimulus to the salesman's psyche.

It is sometimes difficult for a company paying salary to its men to develop a basis for a bonus. The company has chosen salary over other methods of reward for good reasons. We may safely assume other duties than selling are important to it. How then does it measure performance to determine whether a salesman is worth a bonus?

A point system could be the answer. So many points for sales production, so many for each of the other duties a man is expected to perform. Add up the points and the bonus would reflect the value of the salesman's total contribution.

Let's take a look at how such a plan might work. A company could set up a point system as follows:

Job responsibility	*Point potential*	*Salesman A*
Sales production	0–12	10
Opening new accounts	0–6	4
Missionary work	0–4	4
Training new men	0–2	2
Attitude, etc	0–2	1
Maximum point total	26	21

The sales manager evaluates the performance of a salesman and allocates points to him as shown in the second column. The bonus earned would be a percentage of yearly salary according to the following schedule.

Points earned	*Per cent of salary*
Up to 10	—
11–12	1
13–14	2
15–16	4
17–18	6
19–20	8
21–26	10

Please bear in mind that these figures are not offered as recommendations in setting up a bonus plan. They are purely illustrative.

Another observation can be made here. The volume of sales written by a man is a matter of record, so are the number of new accounts he opened and the hours he spent in the field with recruits. The sales manager is on solid ground when allocating points for performance in these areas, but he must rely on subjective judgement when he appraises contribution in the other two segments.

When a bonus is combined with commission all salesmen worth the name are happy, provided the potential for substantial reward is present and demands for the attainment of the bonus are not unreasonable. Many companies paying a bonus to commission men base the award solely on sales production. The fact that the men are on a straight commission indicates that selling is considered to be their primary responsibility.

As we discussed in a previous chapter, each company has its own method of establishing the amount of the bonus a man can earn. Some base it on per cent of target achieved, others on total earnings. In either event the amount will be limited by cost considerations and corporate objectives in the sales area.

A combination of salary, commission and bonus is, from the salesman's point of view, the best of all possible worlds. He has the security of a stable income, the incentive offered by a commission base and the opportunity to increase his income still further by earning a bonus for excelling on the job.

We have emphasized in this chapter the benefits of a fixed bonus rather than a discretionary one. The discretionary type, if used at all, is better suited to fully salaried salesmen than any other class. Salesmen earning at least half their income through commission on sales feel that any bonus paid them should depend on their performance, not the sometimes faulty judgement of executives possibly far removed up the line from them.

Hints to Sales Managers

- When selecting a combination plan don't confine your analysis to expected results only. What might happen is equally important
- As you analyse keep in mind that your scheme should help the company meet its sales objectives. Be sure you know exactly what they are and the effect each component of the scheme will have on them.
- Never forget there are two ways to look at a scheme: from the company's viewpoint and from the salesman's. You work for the company, but the salesmen work under your direction — you have an obligation to them as well as to the company.
- The company and the salesmen are not adversaries. A policy benefiting one at the expense of the other is a bad policy. We'll say it again: the company can succeed only through the success of its employees.

Chapter 9

SALESMEN'S EXPENSES

This is a difficult subject to handle. There are as many types of expenses as there are salesmen and just as many methods of paying them. As the years pass everything seems to have become more complicated and difficult to control. I suppose it's a sign of the times; some people even call it 'progress'.

I vividly remember the first trip I took at company expense. My round trip in a lower berth was paid for and I was given $10 a day for meals and lodging. The $10 was also expected to cover tips and other incidental expenses. The amazing thing was that it did and I came home a couple of dollars ahead of the game.

But times have changed and so have expense accounts. It is difficult to grasp the relationship between corporate expense for sales force compensation and travel and entertainment costs. The method of compensation used by a company will affect the ratio to a marked extent; so will the company's accounting practices. Some lump together all expenses for travelling, by executives as well as the sales force, others don't. Some companies do not differentiate between inside and outside salesmen, others do.

The best I can offer is to say that sales force expenses, as distinct from reward management, can range anywhere from zero to nearly 40 per cent of compensation costs. The zero would of course relate to those companies that pay no expenses, and the maximum probably would apply to employers of a small number of high-quality men who travel the world to sell their products or services.

Eliminating the extremes, we feel safe in suggesting that expenses can average between 20 and 30 per cent of compensation. Companies are naturally concerned with the magnitude of this cost, but that is by no means the only worrisome issue that confronts them. The Inland Revenue is exceedingly strict in its interpretation of what can be classified as a deductible business expense. It takes the attitude that a company can spend its money in any way it wishes provided its shareholders approve, but travel and entertainment costs must conform to established guidelines before they can be deducted on income tax returns.

Regulations cover not only the classification of items that are or are not acceptable as deductions, but also detail the documentation necessary to validate them. Thus, evidence must be presented to demonstrate not only that the expense is of a type and amount allowed, but also that proper receipts prove the money was actually spent.

As a result, companies employing a number of men and women on expense accounts must maintain voluminous and precise records. Individuals must secure receipts and attach them to expense reports submitted to employers for reimbursement. Companies not only have to audit them for accuracy and compliance with company policy, but also to assure that expenses will meet government requirements for deductibility. In addition close watch must be kept on changes in the regulations that affect either the acceptability or validation of expenses.

Thus, when a company reimburses salesmen's expenses it must provide an auditing and accounting staff as well as a legal expert in order to protect its interests. The result is a further increase in costs.

If a company requires its representatives to pay their own expenses it escapes these responsibilities, transferring them to the individuals involved. The general rule is that the party claiming the expense deduction is responsible for adherence to government requirements with respect to deductibility and validation of expenses. This point will come up again and again as we discuss the major options available to a company in handling the travel and entertainment expenses of its sale force.

We'll start by listing a few of the major types of expenses normally incurred by salesmen.

1. Travel — usually by air or car
2. Meals
3. Lodging
4. Entertainment
5. Miscellaneous

Before we go into a discussion of these costs we should talk a little about the types of salesmen that incur them. It is a fact of life that all salesmen are not equal. Some highly educated and trained men earn well in excess of £50,000 a year. Others, just as worthy in their way, drive trucks delivering their products daily to dozens of retail outlets. That is the economic side of the equation.

One breed of salesmen criss-cross the country a dozen times a year, calling on top executives wherever they go. Others find their sales in the square mile of the City of London. Geography plays a major part in determining the amount of expense money they will spend.

So does the social environment in which the salesman operates. For one man a couple of beers at the local pub will suffice to maintain a friendly relationship with a customer, for another *haute cuisine* and vintage wines at the Savoy are *de rigueur*.

The method of reward also plays a role in the handling of expenses. As a general rule, the employer of salaried salesmen is usually responsible for all the business expenses of the men. Salesmen on straight commission customarily pay their expenses out of generous commission rates. Various plans are used when a man's compensation combines salary and commission.

Merchandisers paid by salary usually receive a fixed expense allowance or the company picks up all the tabs. Here I refer to the man who delivers breakfast cereals and racks the boxes in the supermarket, the actual order having been written by a sales executive at the buying office of the chain.

At this point we'll examine in some detail the most widely used methods of handling salesmen's expenses.

Expenses Paid by Salesmen

When a salesman pays his own expenses it is unnecessary for the company to maintain any records nor does its auditor have to check the amount or legitimacy of an expenditure. The result is a substantial saving for a company employing a number of men, but this method of handling expenses is not an unmixed blessing to the employer.

Commission rates must be increased by an amount sufficient to cover the individual's costs. This is not as easy as it sounds. Costs of food and lodging vary in different parts of the country and fluctuate even in adjacent territories. One salesman with a small compact area to cover is home every night and drives no more than 10,000 miles a year calling on his customers. Another sleeps away from home three or four nights a week and drives 40,000 miles a year in covering his territory. The company cannot have a different commission schedule for every man, so an arbitrary adjustment is made in rates. Some men will profit, others may lose, but what else can be done?

A further complication results when sales fluctuate. In good times not all the rate increase is devoted to paying expenses; the salesman profits, at times substantially. Conversely, when a salesman's production falls for any of a number of reasons, he is reluctant to spend his money on any but essential expenses. He is inclined to cut out entertaining that might be important to the company and skimps in any way he can. He might even decide not to make trips that should be made. A further decrease in sales costs him as much as the company, but that is what some men will do to save a few pounds of their money.

By losing control of expense money the company also loses control over the spending habits of its men. Staid and prestigious companies do not approve when their representatives stay at third or fourth rate hotels and drive around in eight-year-old, battered heaps.

How does a salesman regard a policy under which he pays his expenses? In the first place the necessity of maintaining exact records is transferred to him. In order to deduct business expenses, he must satisfy the Inland Revenue that the money was actually spent and that it was spent for purposes allowed by the regulations. Furthermore he must be able to produce evidence in the form of receipts to verify his expenditures. Some men will attempt to beat the system, but should a day of reckoning arrive, the salesman will have more pressing duties than selling his company's products until the misunderstanding is cleared up.

It is safe to say that men will be more conservative spending their own money than if it is company largesse they are dispensing.

So much for the chap who pays his own expenses. We'll shift to the other end of the spectrum — the man whose expenses are fully paid by the company.

Expenses Paid by Company

Travel

First of all the salesman must understand exactly what expenses his employer deems proper. On plane trips a company might permit travel only at coach rate. Men of higher status might be permitted to enjoy business-class accommodations, and even first class if they are home office moguls. Whatever the rules are on air travel, they must be made clear to the salesman.

The same is true for lodging. Many companies establish allowable rate levels for different areas of the country. A room in the West End of London costs more than one in Glasgow. For that matter, so does a meal. In many parts of the country a guideline of £20 a day for meals would allow a man to eat like a king, but if he were in London and enjoyed a full English breakfast as well as lunch he might not have too much left for his evening meal.

Other Expenses

Let's assume the company reaches an understanding with its salesmen on travel, lodging and meals. How about other necessary expenses like laundry and valet services? The widely prevalent theory is that the salesman should expect the company to pay all expenses he would not incur provided he was at home. Well, laundry must get done wherever you are and suits need pressing when you have been caught in an afternoon shower. Some companies authorize laundry and cleaning expenses only if a man is away for a week or more. Others, more graciously, allow them at all times.

What about a taxi from the airport into town instead of the shuttle bus? Whatever the company policy, it should be clearly understood by the salesmen.

May a salesman phone home in the evening to learn if the boiler or the air conditioner has been repaired or to find how Linda did on the spelling test? I should hope so, but let company policy be a matter of record.

The general rule is that a person should be able to continue his normal living habits while travelling on an expense account. His standard should be neither above nor below what he is accustomed to at home. That is a good rule that should be agreeable to both the company and the salesman.

How about entertaining? The company expects a certain amount of it from its men. Dinner and theatre tickets can cost a small fortune, but being too cheap can cost even more in customer relations. Judgement is the key and company policy should establish guidelines.

Now, a word about record keeping. Companies have forms for recording expenses if they have more than one or two individuals on expense accounts. Reports must be presented to the company before reimbursement is made. That is one report salesmen are not reluctant to prepare.

The reports must be checked to see if the salesman's arithmetic passes muster, but also to determine if expenditures are for authorized purposes and are not excessive in amount. In addition receipts will be reviewed to determine if they conform with government requirements that will make them acceptable as deductible company expenses.

At times it is difficult for a salesman to finance a lengthy trip out of his own pocket. Many companies authorize a permanent advance to a man, a fund that will be reimbursed when a man's expense account is approved. If a salesman handles this money through his personal bank account there is always the possibility that company funds will at times be devoted to other uses than those intended.

Bear this in mind: control does not connote stinginess. It does imply that company policies are to be followed, that unauthorized expenditures will not be honoured and that padding will be detected and dealt with. Well-adjusted men content with their jobs and their compensation are not overly inclined to juggle their expense accounts.

What effect does payment of all travelling expenses have on a company? It makes it difficult to control selling expenses or even to budget for them accurately. Perhaps knowing that the company will pick up the tab begets an extravagant attitude on the part of salesmen who have no incentive to economize. Finally, the office staff and the sales manager must have sharp eyes to police expense accounts and to spot seemingly unnecessary trips to the scene of popular football matches.

Interestingly, company policies on expenses are more often too liberal rather than too tough. The reason is that companies know the effect on sales when they are constantly feuding, at times acrimoniously, with men about questionable expense account items.

Salesmen are relieved that their responsibility ends when the company accepts their expense accounts. If the tax collector has a complaint, the dispute is between him and the company, not the salesman. The salesman also enjoys a sense of security. His expenses are not controlled by his sales volume and he cannot be made responsible for any expenditures provided they were consistent with company policy.

The company finds record keeping and auditing expensive. Also, salesmen's expenses fall into the fixed classification — they maintain their constant course whether sales rise or fall. This is a disadvantage to a company in slack periods.

On the plus side, the company can control the activities of its men. It knows where they have been, what they were doing, which would not have been the case if the men paid their own expenses and went where they pleased. When a company pays a man's expenses his earnings are not affected and payroll deductions and taxes are not involved. The expense is handled like any other profit-and-loss item on the company's statement.

Fixed Expense Allowance

Under this plan the company avoids the record keeping and auditing required when it pays a representative's expenses. Consider it this way: when a company reimburses a salesman for his expenses, it assumes the responsibility of justifying them to state or federal government auditors. They are the company's expenses, not the salesman's. When the company does not reimburse expenses directly, the salesman is responsible for validating them on his tax returns.

Under a fixed expense-allowance plan the company pays a man an agreed amount for each day, week or month to cover the expenses he is expected to incur. The allowance paid is added to the man's earnings and necessary deductions are taken from it. The salesman then claims his actual expenses as deductions on his tax returns. The allowance might vary from £10 a day to £5,000 or more a month and a cheque will be issued at designated intervals.

You will observe that this plan has many similarities to the one under which a commission salesman is paid at a higher rate and is responsible for his expenses. The only real difference is that under the allowance method the man receives a fixed sum hand-tailored to his needs, rather than a higher return on sales. The added commission a man receives, depending as it does on sales volume, is a variable expense to the company. A continuing allowance is a fixed expense, not affected by fluctuations in sales.

Let's see how a fixed-allowance plan might work.

Salesman	*Days away*	*Lodging (£35/night)*	*Meals (£25/day)*	*Lunch (£6)*	*Misc*	*Total*
A	3	105	75	12	10	202
B	1	35	50	18	60	163

Salesman A has a widespread territory and his regular schedule requires him to be away from home three nights a week. He can get a room in a comfortable hotel for £35 a night. His food allowance of £25 a day while he is away will allow him to eat well and even have a drink before dinner. The company generously allows him £6 for lunch on the days he will return home at night. Some employers feel, and who can deny the equity of their attitude, that when the man leaves home for work and returns in time for dinner he is no different from the ordinary office worker who buys his lunch every day. Yet, the company includes two lunches in the allocation.

Salesman A is not expected to entertain customers in the normal course of his activity so he receives £10 weekly for miscellaneous expenses such as tolls, parking and the like. On special occasions when he finds it necessary to entertain, he submits a receipt for the expense and hopes to receive reimbursement.

Salesman B has a different-sized territory which requires him to be away only a single night a week. On the other hand, his customers are such that he does receive a regular allocation for entertaining.

You will note that up to this point we have said nothing about automobile expenses. No, they have not been forgotten; they are so important we will devote a special section of the chapter to them.

A fixed expense allowance is good for a company provided sales management is firmly in control of the sales force. Allowances must be set only after a full study has been made of the travel pattern of each man and the varying costs of food and lodging in each territory. Activity of each man must be closely monitored: is he actually doing what his schedule calls for, making the trips he is scheduled to make? Managers must be alert to changes and make timely adjustments in allowances when necessary.

Under this method of expense reimbursement a salesman may be reluctant to seek new accounts at a distance from one of his regular stops. He might even attempt to increase his income by using the telephone rather than calling on a distant customer.

The company's work load is reduced in record keeping and auditing.

Whether selling expenses will be higher or lower and more or less effectively utilized than they would be under another method of payment depends on the ability of the sales manager to set allowances accurately and his complete knowledge of what his men are actually doing in the field.

Expense Allowances Based on Sales

Companies may employ another means of making an expense allowance to its salesmen, by which a man would receive 3 or 4 per cent of his total sales amount to cover his expenses. This method offers two major advantages to an employer. It relieves the company of the necessity of maintaining any expense account records, since the allowance is added to the salesman's earnings and it is his responsibility to validate his deductions. Secondly, selling expenses become a variable expense rather than a fixed charge. The company pays a salesman a percentage of gross sales it can afford and as far as it is concerned, that is the end of the matter.

Some salesmen will make a substantial profit out of such a deal; others might have to dig into their own pockets if their particular selling expenses are high. To be as equitable as possible the company should set a rate for each salesman or perhaps each class of salesman, but this is seldom if ever possible. Many variables make accurate solution of inherent problems difficult to achieve. One man sells high-volume, low-margin products, another low-volume, high-margin ones. The man in one territory might sell 90 per cent of his business to a handful of customers located within an hour's drive of home. Another salesman must spend all week on the road to get modest orders from dozens of accounts.

Inequities are inevitable under this system. The amount of expense allowance is made purely a function of sales volume, but actual expenses incurred might be controlled by a half-dozen other factors, all more relevant than sales.

Combination Plans

It is not unusual for a company to pay actual costs of travel and lodging and make a fixed allowance for meals and other expenses. The company's record keeping is confined to plane tickets and hotel or motel costs. Both are easy to document. The salesman takes care of all other evidences of payment. The establishment of the amount of the fixed allowance follows the procedure already outlined.

Another method often used to reimburse salesmen for other than travelling cost sets one per diem rate for men at home and another when they are on the road. Such a system eliminates much of the inequity involved in a fixed-rate allowance plan under which a salesman receives an amount based on estimates of where his time will be spent.

Per diems will vary in parallel with local prices. In one area £60 will cover lodging, meals and miscellaneous charges adequately, in another £100 might not be sufficient. A per diem plan will allow the company to exert some amount of control over expenses and the activities of its men.

If a man is working his home area he might be allowed £10 a day for incidentals. Entertainment costs can be built into a per diem, but if the company so elects it can require its salesmen to list their entertainment costs on a special report. Under this system the company has greater control over the expenses.

Summary

Before we go into automobile expenses and how they can be handled we'll add a chart covering the plusses and minuses from the salesman's and company's viewpoint of the various methods of paying expenses that we have discussed.

Payment of Expenses

From salesman's viewpoint	From company's viewpoint
SALESMAN PAYS	
Records are required to support expense deductions on tax records	No records required Higher commission rate is a variable expense
More money is available in good times, less in bad, yet expenses continue on an almost even keel	Little control over salesman's comings and goings possible Plan does not differentiate between costs in various territories
It is possible to skimp on standards of living when away from home and thereby increase disposable income	The plan cannot be equitable to all men
Some men profit from increased commission rates and some lose out depending on travel demands of different territories	

Payment of Expenses *(continued)*

From salesman's viewpoint	From company's viewpoint
EXPENSES PAID BY COMPANY	
No records need be kept by salesmen other than those required to secure reimbursement from company An extravagant attitude may develop in minds of salesmen	Clear-cut company policy is essential covering allowable expenses. Similar precise explanation of acceptable limits for food, lodging and so forth is necessary. Policies should reflect full understanding of costs throughout the area. Voluminous and exact records must be kept. Expense reports must be examined to prevent padding or inclusion of unauthorized items. The company has diminished control over salesmen's expenses as long as they conform with company policy The company has greater control over the activities of its men as it has a full record of their travels and calls
FIXED EXPENSE ALLOWANCE	
Salesmen must keep records to support tax deductions Receiving a fixed allowance with no reporting required by the company might encourage men not to do the travelling on which the allowance is based If allowance is not soundly developed, inequities are bound to result	No record keeping or auditing required Allowance is included in salesman's earnings and handled the same as salary or commission Administration of the plan requires analysis of each salesman's travel schedule Each allowance should be accurately figured. Many opportunities exist for mistakes. Changes are necessary when the customer base shifts in a territory

Payment of Expenses *(continued)*

From salesman's viewpoint	From company's viewpoint
FIXED EXPENSE ALLOWANCE	
	Men on fixed allowance are reluctant to stray away from normal routine of calls, thus opening new accounts may not be given proper attention
	In general costs are fixed rather than variable
EXPENSE ALLOWANCE BASED ON SALES	
Salesmen must keep records for tax purposes	No record keeping or auditing required
Plan is not equitable to all men. Some territories are more or less expensive to cover than others.	Expenses are variable, not fixed
	Plan bases allowance on sales, which may have little to do with actual expenses
	Does not differentiate between high-volume, low-margin and low-volume, high-margin sales
COMBINATION PLANS	
Company pays travel and lodging, salesman receives fixed allowance for other expenses	
Salesman must keep records for tax purposes	So must company, although to a lesser extent
Salesman cannot spend a week at home phoning customers without company's knowledge. This would have been possible under a fixed allowance plan.	Makes fixed allowance much simpler to figure, yet problems of equity remain
	Expenses are semi-controllable
	Company does know where men have or have not been
Company pays travel and sets per diem amount for other expenses	
Salesman must keep records	Company record keeping minimal
More equitable than fixed-allowance plan as it is more closely tied to men's activities	Per diem allowance is more accurate than fixed-allowance plan

Payment of Expenses *(continued)*

From salesman's viewpoint	From company's viewpoint
COMBINATION PLANS	
	Company has greater knowledge of sales force activity and can exert greater control over it

Automobile Expenses

Three categories of cars are used by salesmen: company owned, leased and salesman owned. We'll discuss each in order.

Company-Owned Cars

The mechanics go like this. The company buys a car, pays the licence fee, pays the insurance premiums and turns the car over to a salesman. When the car has outlived its usefulness the company disposes of it and buys another for the man. While the salesman has it the company pays for petrol, oil, tyres, maintenance and repairs when needed.

The company keeps depreciation records on each car and when it is ultimately sold either a profit or a loss is booked on the transaction. Company expenses fall into two groups: fixed and variable. Once the depreciation is set up it is a fixed expense, so are insurance and licence fees. Such costs are paid even if the car is never used.

Variable expenses include petrol, oil, tyres, maintenance and so forth, all of which are controlled by the number of miles the car is driven. Many companies replace cars after three years or 60,000 miles, whichever comes first.

Let's take a look at this from the company's point of view. Record keeping is voluminous and costly. Individual records are kept on each vehicle and if a company has a large fleet, a section must be created in the accounting department to handle them. The purchase cost of cars is held down by discounts available to fleet buyers.

It would be a mistake not to mention the investment angle with regard to company-owned cars. A company needs substantial resources to buy 100 or 1,000 cars. Of course they aren't all bought at the same time; a fleet turns over about 30 per cent a year. Still, fifty cars cost a pretty penny. Have you bought even one lately?

How does a company determine whether it gets its money's worth out of a car it supplies to a salesman? First we'll estimate the annual fixed costs. If a car will be depreciated over three years and we throw in the other fixed costs, we find the annual fixed expense can reach £3,000 to £4,000. Of course the make and model of the cars purchased will have a major effect on this total, as will the area of the country where they are registered. For the sake of simplicity we'll use the figure of £3,000 for our example. The costs of operating might average around 12 pence a mile.

If a salesman drives the car 10,000 miles, the cost to the company is 30 pence a mile for fixed costs plus 12 pence for variable ones, a total of 42 pence a mile. At 20,000 miles the total would be 27 pence a mile — fifteen pence fixed plus 12 pence variable. At 30,000 miles the total costs would drop to 22 pence.

A company would be prudent to prepare a chart using the appropriate figures and superimpose on it the results that would obtain should the company rent its cars or require salesmen to provide their own. We'll have a try at this later in the chapter.

We can say that the more mileage a salesman puts on a company car, the more economical will it be for the company to own it. How the costs will compare with other types of ownership need to be determined before a company decides how to handle transportation of its sales force. So much for the financial side.

The company can choose the make and model of the cars it provides for its men. It can arrange for a distinctive paint job on its cars and even for advertising on the body if it wishes. The company, if it is concerned with the image it wishes to project, can control the age and appearance of the cars used by its men.

Salesmen like driving company-owned cars. They don't have to worry about any of the costs of ownership — putting out their own funds and then hoping to get a square deal from the company. Having someone else totally responsible is a comforting thought.

Leased Cars

Companies leasing cars for salesmen escape much of the record keeping that goes along with ownership. Makes and models can be selected, used as long as desired and then returned to the leaser with no need to dispose of the discards. The company also escapes the requirement to lay out large sums to buy cars.

Leasing companies are in business to make money — don't ignore that fact. They must do all the clerical work a company would have to do if it owned the cars; they have to buy and pay for the cars they lease. Leasing rates are set high enough to cover costs and return a profit. Thus it would appear that leasing its fleet would be more expensive to a company than owning it. Yet many companies are content to pay the premium to avoid the large investment and the administrative requirements that accompany ownership.

It makes no difference to a salesman whether he drives a leased car or a company-owned one. As long as he doesn't have to pay for the car he doesn't care who does.

Salesman-Owned Cars

We have already determined that it is not economic for a company to buy or lease cars for a group of salesmen who will not use them extensively. Owning or leasing cars is good business for a company when its men put high mileage on them, bad business when mileage is low.

When a salesman drives his own car the company has no control over either its age or appearance. Some salesmen are proud of their cars and keep them in tip-top condition, to others a car is merely a means of transportation and it suits them as long as it runs.

A salesman's principal worry is whether the company will grant him a car allowance sufficient to cover his operating costs with enough over to buy a new car to replace one near the end of its useful life. If the allowance is generous, an economy-minded man might cover expenses and have a little cushion left. If it is on the stingy side, a salesman will be resentful.

Now we'll consider how a company can reimburse its men driving company or leased cars for petrol and normal upkeep charges and make equitable payment to men using personal cars on company business.

Reimbursement for Car Expenses

The simplest plan and the easiest to administer a company can adopt is to pay one fixed mileage rate on cars it owns or rents and a higher fixed rate to salesmen who drive their own cars. Unfortunately, simplicity is not necessarily a synonym for equity. Maintenance costs vary in different parts of the country. Even petrol cost differs substantially in different areas.

The variation in costs is even wider when we consider fixed costs such as the insurance a salesman must pay if he drives his car on company business. Insurance damage rates can double from one area to another.

A company owning or leasing cars usually reimburses salesmen for all normal maintenance and operating costs. Since petrol and oil are included in this category the salesman presents his receipts and is reimbursed. Many men carry a company credit card and the bills are submitted directly to the company. The theory is simple — when the company supplies the car, the company picks up all the bills. No problem there. Problems do arise when the salesman owns the car. There are a number of ways he can collect his expenses.

Payment based on mileage.
A company may pay a man 27 pence a mile to compensate him for the use of his car. Such a payment presents no administrative problems to the employer. The salesman lists the mileage for each trip he makes and the company pays him. Salesmen who do extensive business driving, 30,000 miles or more a year, like this system of reimbursement. The reason is clear — they make money. Actual operating costs average around 12 pence a mile leaving 15 pence a mile to pay fixed charges. Thus, if a salesman drives 30,000 miles, he receives £4,500 toward these expenses which, depending on what make and model car he drives, might not exceed £3,500. On the other hand, the salesman who drives only 10,000 miles on company business would receive only £1,500 to cover fixed costs, which would leave him deep in a hole.

Salesmen know what they are going to receive. They might not like it but at least they know. Companies are able to estimate closely the payments they will make, so budgeting problems are reduced.

The major weakness of this method of reimbursing salesmen is that it is inequitable.

Fixed sum payment plus mileage.
This method avoids the weakness of the straight-mileage plan. Under it a salesman receives a fixed amount each month. £250 for example, plus 12 pence per mile driven. Each man is thus assured of £3,000 a year to cover fixed costs. His mileage allowance should take care of his normal operating expenses.

But what about the man who uses his car only occasionally on company business and at least half of its annual mileage is attributable to family use? In such cases the company would reduce his fixed allowance to £125 a month and mileage would be paid only for the distance covered while on company business.

In this connection, we might mention that companies are usually generous in permitting reasonable personal use of company-owned or rented vehicles that are driven extensively on company business. More often than not they pay all operating and maintenance expenses, even though the salesman may put 1,000 miles or so on the car each year dropping the children off at school or doing the grocery shopping. Expenses incurred while on extended vacation trips might be handled differently.

Sliding scale mileage rates.
This method seeks to achieve results similar to those obtained from a fixed allowance plus mileage plan. A salesman might be paid 27 pence a mile for

the first 12,000 miles he drives, 20 pence on the next 12,000 and 15 pence on the excess over 24,000 miles. If he drove 30,000 miles in a year his payment would work out like this.

First	12,000 miles at 27 pence	=	£3,240
Next	12,000 miles at 20 pence	=	2,400
Final	6,000 miles at 15 pence	=	900
Total	30,000		£6,540
Operating expenses at 12 pence			3,600
Contribution to fixed charges			£2,940

Results are satisfactory to a salesman who drives 30,000 miles a year. If his territory was such that he need put only 15,000 miles on his mileometer, he would receive £2,040 to cover fixed costs.

It must be recognized that when we use £3,000 as an estimate of fixed costs and 12 pence a mile as an operating expense figure we do not expect you to consider them as anything but examples to show the calculations involved. The actual costs will need to be carefully determined in each case, and re-calculated at regular intervals; as inflation invalidates them. The Automobile Association (AA) probably produces the best set of guidelines for UK car operating costs. In addition, actual figures will vary with the make and model of the cars involved, the fluctuations in the cost of petrol and tyres, the replacement costs of automobiles and the cost of insurance needed to cover the owners of the cars.

There is no one best way to reimburse a salesman for the use of his car on company business. Some companies get around the problem by simply increasing commission rates and telling the salesman to provide his own transportation. A cop-out? Perhaps, but think of the record keeping and auditing a company avoids, the hassles it escapes with men who are dissatisfied with their allowances. Of course, a lot would depend on the commission or salary adjustment. If a salesman's total compensation, after deducting for his car expense, is competitive and adequately rewards him for his production, neither he nor the company should have any basis for complaint.

The following graph projects company costs under several methods of handling car expense. We are staying with our choices of £3,000 fixed expense and 12 pence a mile variable cost. Rental costs are not included; we assume they would at least equal and probably exceed the £3,000 figure. It is hoped that managers able to secure actual company costs can tailor the graph to the actual conditions in their company and the adjusted chart would indicate in what direction they should proceed.

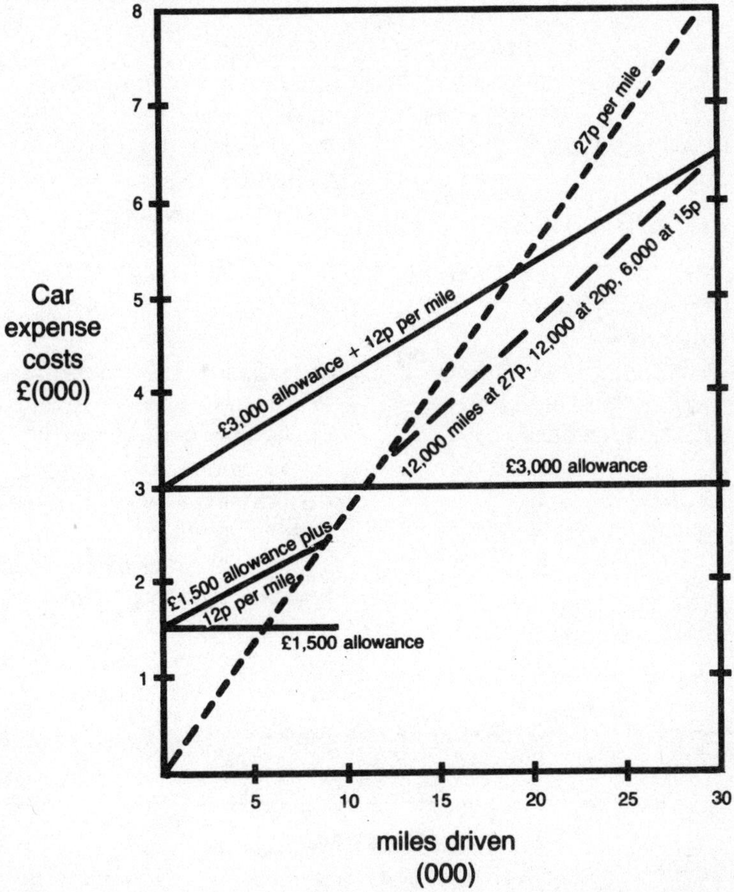

Payment schedule	*10,000 miles*	*20,000 miles*	*30,000 miles*
27p per mile	£2,700	£5,400	£8,100
£3,000 fixed plus 12p per mile	4,200	5,400	6,600
27p first 12,000 miles 20p next 12,000 miles 15p additional 6,000 miles	2,700	4,840	6,540
£1,500 fixed plus 12p per mile	2,700	N A	N A

Car Expenses

From salesman's viewpoint	From company's viewpoint
OWNED OR RENTED CARS	
Salesman pleased when company pays all expenses and will replace car when required	Company controls age and condition of cars Company obligated for large fixed expenses Administrative expenses high
SALESMAN-OWNED CARS	
High-milage salesmen prefer flat mileage rate Low-mileage men prefer fixed allowance plus mileage to cover operating expenses All approve sliding scale mileage rates, provided they are adequate	No control over age and appearance of cars Fixed mileage rate is easiest to administer, but excessively costly when mileage is high Option of increasing salary or commission rate to cover car costs is alternative Costs are easier to calculate and forecast. Administrative costs are minimized. Fixed allowance plus mileage is equitable and cost efficient

Hints to Sales Managers

- Whatever plan you adopt to cover salesman's expenses, make sure it is thoroughly understood by your men.
- Be familiar with the travel routines of your men. Determine what lodging and meals cost throughout your territory.
- Don't be a penny-pincher, but don't make yourself an easy mark for your sales force.
- Get in the habit of checking where your men are going by studying their expense reports
- Is your expense policy more or less liberal than those of leading competitors? If so, why?
- Analyse your company's car expense policy. Are some men treated better than others? Can the imbalance be corrected?

Chapter 10

TERRITORIES

There are other areas that must be discussed before we go about setting up a sample reward scheme. The first of these is territories.

Many companies learned early on that it was necessary to establish clearly defined territories, not only for district offices but also for individual salesmen. Yet, this is not universally so. To a number of industries a wide-open policy is not only preferable but essential. Insurance salesmen, estate agents and other personal service organizations could not function effectively if strict territorial limits were enforced. Personal relationships are of paramount importance in those professions and such relationships know no geographical boundaries. Thus a man or woman in such a business must be free to sell wherever customers can be found. It is also true that in the high-tech industries the man best qualified to handle a specific account is assigned to it regardless of where the account is located.

No substantial administrative problems should be encountered when a territory is considered open to all the representatives operating in it. If a lead is received the manager gives it to the next name on the list. Bad feelings can develop if the manager shows favouritism in passing out leads or, what is worse, claims office sales as his own, but a man who would do that probably has other failings as well and won't be around very long.

Despite the exceptions noted, the vast majority of companies do find the territorial concept the best approach to the marketing function. Districts are established and men assigned to well-defined segments of them. Ordinarily they have exclusive rights to all sales made in their territory.

It is inevitable that as time goes on territories, as well as men, change. In addition, territorial boundaries must be fixed when a company expands into a new area. Thus, organization and reorganization of territories is an ongoing function of sales management and an understanding of these two functions is required when establishing or modifying reward schemes in areas where territories are being restructured. Consequently we'll spend a few pages on the subject.

Territory Evaluation

When we consider the word *territory* we usually think in terms of geography. Northwest Territory has a romantic ring about it, as does Yukon Territory. Towering firs and broad rivers in one, snow capped mountains and rivers of ice in the other.

In a selling sense territory means something quite different. The sales executive thinks in terms of people, customers to whom he can sell his goods or services, rather than areas on a map. He cannot, however, ignore geography. His potential customers are not herded together for him in a convenient bundle waiting for a salesman to descend on them. They are scattered across the map and if the sales manager is to make them profitable customers, he must find an economic way to get his salesmen inside their purchasing departments.

Some territories are like abandoned gold mines. Chemical analysis has disclosed that gold is present, but the cost of extraction is greater than the value of the gold extracted. The trick is to secure sales at a low-enough cost that a profit can be made from them.

There are many information sources available to a company seeking to decide whether it might be profitable to move into a new area. Census information is available in a variety of forms from the Stationery Office, and there are also a number of specialist consultancies which have processed these raw data into forms more directly useful to sales managers; presented as 'sales bricks', for example. Chambers of Commerce are always ready to supply information on factories and wholesale or retail establishments located in the area. Local authorities can be helpful along the same line.

A company wishing to expand will examine the information it accumulates and pick an area that looks promising. If it is cautious, it will take a number of steps before sending in two or three men and preparing to handle the flood of orders they are expected to produce. The more it knows about a territory the better is the chance for a successful expansion. Let us list a number of the points a sales manager would consider in deciding whether it would pay his company to expand into a particular area.

1. The number of possible customers in the area. Break them down into classifications: large, medium-sized, small.
2. The location of possible customers. Are they concentrated in one or more clearly defined locations or scattered through the area?
3. The potential value of the entire market in the area.
4. The calibre of the competition that will be encountered. How many competitors are there? What is the quality of their products or services? What is a realistic assessment of your chances of enticing customers away from them?

5. The share of market you should be able to achieve and how long it will take to attain it.
6. The work load required to cover the territory. At this point the sales manager pulls out his maps, plugs in his calculator and sharpens his pencils. He is about to make a preliminary route schedule for covering the territory. He has already decided on the number of prospects to be called on, broken them down into those where one call a month will suffice, others to be called on twice a month and a few that should be visited every week. From the list he determines the number of calls to be made each month. He already knows company standards for average time spent on calls so total time is easily computed. Travel time is roughly estimated from the routes he has sketched out, added to call time and a total is arrived at. It is quickly apparent how many men will be required to cover the territory. Perhaps the study reveals that three men are needed. Undaunted the sales manager passes along to the final point.
7. Comparison of costs of manning the territory with sales to be expected from it. Three men, let us say, will cost the company £75,000 a year in rewards plus an additional £20,000 for expenses. It is not to be expected that sales in the first year, at least, will be of sufficient volume to cover this substantial investment. The sales manager refers back to his estimate under item 5 and compares it with projected costs. Is the risk of going in with three men worth taking, or would it be more prudent to start with a single man covering a much smaller and more concentrated group of potential customers? If that were done and the man proved successful, coverage could be expanded by assignment of one or more trainees to the area at a later date.

The sales manager makes up his mind, calls the boss at the home office and tells him the results of his study. He asks for and receives authority to proceed as he proposed. One up for him. Let us hope his decision was sound. It was, provided his analysis was thorough and his estimates reasonably attainable.

Opening New Territories

Choice of the right man is essential when a company decides to open a territory. If it is an area previously covered by manufacturer's reps or distributors, the chosen man will at least have a base of customers to build on. If it is virgin territory, he will have to start from scratch.

Ideally the man chosen will be confident, experienced and convinced that the opportunity offered him is sufficiently great that he will be able to achieve and surpass his earnings goal. It will be a big advantage if he is one of those rare individuals who is constantly concerned with improving his lot in life. The sales manager will attempt to find a man who is amenable to direction, receptive to help offered from the district office. He should have demonstrated ability in opening new accounts, missionary work and meeting the public in general. Above all he will be no stranger to hard work and willing to locate in what is to him a new part of the country.

If the company is fortunate enough to discover a man with these attributes, it must treat him as he deserves to be treated. He should be guaranteed his average earnings during the previous year or two for a period sufficient for him to build his earnings from the new territory to that figure. Further, he should be a continuing concern of his sales manager while he is developing his business.

An effective sales manager should do everything he can to ease the path of a salesman opening a new territory. He will already have pin-pointed the principal prospective customers, know their probable needs and will have learned the names of purchasing department heads. He might have made appointments for a 'get-acquainted' visit and he will be sure to accompany the salesman on his first trip through the territory.

Coddling? Not a bit of it. It is as important to the sales manager as it is to the salesman to get the enterprise off to a good start. Making a trip with the salesman provides an opportunity for the manager to establish rapport with him, demonstrate an interest in and concern for him. Few individuals are so mentally strong they can sail into a new job in unfamiliar surroundings without appreciating the presence and encouragement of a friendly ally, particularly if that ally is the boss. Consideration is a quality much appreciated by everyone and a personal relationship can be an important bond between a sales manager and his men.

Territorial Realignment

Let us discuss redefinition of an existing territory. First of all, why should a territory be tampered with? Perhaps the area has enjoyed unusually rapid growth; many businesses including a number of potential customers have moved in. As a result the market for a particular company may have expanded substantially.

The salesman in the territory may have grown too, but not at a pace equal to the region he covers. On the other hand, he may have become complacent, content to skim the cream off the top and neglect other responsibilities such as missionary work and soliciting new accounts. But, even the best salesman, working as hard as he can, may not be able to provide adequate service to everyone in his territory. He may be doing his best, but that is not good enough.

Should the territory have grown to the extent that it can support a second man, he should be put in and the territory divided between the two. Should an adjoining territory be subject to the same conditions and should neither be able to support a second man, a third territory with acceptable potential could be created from sections of each existing territory.

In either situation attention should be given to the reward scheme of all the men involved in the switch. The resident salesman who has lost a substantial percentage of his accounts should be protected while he develops his smaller territory more effectively. It will take him time to bring his earnings up to average, perhaps six months or even a year. During the selected period he could be guaranteed his average earnings over the equal preceding period. The same arrangement could be made available to the man moved into the newly formed territory.

At the beginning of the changeover it would be important for the old salesman to introduce the new man to the accounts he inherits. The fact that his earnings are protected during the changeover should make him more willing to perform this important task. Of course, the sales manager would have the responsibility of seeing that both men, old and new, got off to a good start.

It is one of the immutable facts of salesmanship that a man will earn what he wants to earn — provided, of course, that the sales potential is there. He will do this even though he really has to exert himself in a relatively poor territory. Likewise, in the richest of territories many men will work just hard enough to meet their earnings goal. Some men are £20,000 a year men, others £30,000, still others £50,000. No matter where they are, their inclination is to earn that amount and little more. Why is this? Who knows, but it is a fact. One of the toughest jobs a sales manager has is to develop a £30,000 man into a £40,000 man. Success in such an endeavour is one of the greatest rewards he can experience.

What we have said here goes for a surprisingly large number of salesmen, but fortunately not for all of them. There is a group of highly motivated men whose constant goal is to do better for themselves and their families, who consider their present jobs not as an end, but merely as stepping stones in their path to the top. These are the individuals who lift themselves by their own bootstraps through earnings plateaus into the upper echelon of management. More power to them: they deserve everything they achieve.

At times the potential of a territory outgrows the aspirations of a salesman, but not to the extent that dividing the territory is justified. More satisfactory results might be obtained by switching assignments so that territorial potential is more in line with the earnings objectives of the salesmen.

Territories sometimes lose rather than gain in potential. Industrial customers close factories or reduce output. Changes in technology make some end products obsolete with the result that a territory, no matter how adequately covered, can no longer support a salesman even of a low earning capacity. The only alternative a company has is to break up the territory and assign segments to adjacent ones. The displaced salesman can be moved to a different area. Should the drop in potential be severe enough that continued coverage is not profitable under normal selling policy, the company might consider using manufacturer's reps or distributors to service existing accounts.

Matching Territories with Men

This is a serious subject and should not be treated lightly, but before we go into a discussion of the matter let's allow our fancy to take over for a minute or two. We'll start by assuming that a corporation develops a group of products totally unlike its regular line and decides to market them in twelve territories. A like number of salesmen are transferred to the new division. The sales executive in charge of the project has the problem of assigning one of the men to each of the territories.

He approaches the task with misgivings. Should salesman A be placed in territory 4 or should he be assigned to number 6, and number 4 given to salesman B? He wonders how many possible combinations of men and territories there can be.

Having earned an MBA from one of the major business schools, he recalls the principles of linear programming, the science of quantifying combinations and permutations. A few minutes of key punching on his computer reveals the awful truth to him: there are exactly 479,001,600 possible assignments in placing twelve men in twelve territories. It's a fact. If you don't believe me, ask any mathematically-minded friend to check the figure.

Our harried executive doubts he has the time to explore and analyse each option, but he must make a decision, and soon. His first action is to switch off the computer, then pick up a pencil and get to work on a scratch pad.

He lists the characteristics of each territory as he perceives it and does the same for the dozen men assigned to him. The more he knows of the men and the area, the better will be his judgement in making assignments.

The following chart suggests a few of the points he will consider. The sales executive will add many more and go into as much detail as he can with the information at his disposal. Basically:

Territories can be:	Salesmen can be:
Good, poor, average	Good, poor, average
Of different shapes, sizes, terrain or climate	Young, old, experienced, inexperienced
Principally urban or rural	Climbing the ladder or sliding down
Varied in sales potential	Of different types; suited to city dwelling or country selling
Varied in number and size of possible accounts	Of different personalities; leaders, followers, highly motivated, relatively unambitious plodders, fiercely independent or amenable to direction and control
Subject to special or unusual economic conditions	Skimmers or diligent in performing all the prescribed functions of their jobs
Strongly or poorly covered by competition	

When his lists are complete, the manager starts to fill square holes with square pegs, round ones with round pegs. Many assignments will be obviously right, a few might be open to question, but time constraints do not permit our executive to check even a paltry 10 million or so possible alternatives. He makes his assignments and that is the end of the matter for the time being. If his preparation and analysis were thorough his decisions will have been wise ones.

Mismatches of Territories and Men

It frequently becomes apparent that mismatches exist in a district. One man might be working like a Trojan in a poor territory producing an unexpectedly high percentage of potential, yet not yet be able to earn the return his efforts justify. Another man might earn much more, despite working at a more leisurely pace because of the richness of his territory. Here are a few instances where reassigning men might be justified.

1. An up-and-coming tiger is trapped in a territory with low potential. His advancement is blocked because of the lack of opportunity. Why not replace him with a new man still on salary or drawing account? It might be an excellent location for him to learn the business.

The present incumbent could be shifted to a territory more compatible with his talents.

2. A territory with good and still growing potential is covered by a plodder, content with present earnings who cannot be motivated to develop further the sales opportunities available.
   Why not transfer him to a mature territory of limited growth potential? He can be expected to continue to do the job he has done in the past and that is all the territory needs. Sales will not drop nor will his earnings. At the same time a man on the way up who deserves a chance to show what he can do could be put in his place.
3. A territory might be small, compact, well developed, but of limited potential. It would make an excellent spot for an older, still effective man close to retirement. Put him in the territory and reassign the present incumbent.

In general, an analysis of men and territories may disclose that there are mismatches. Superior men can have inferior territories. Switching men would seem warranted if the company had the normal objective of increasing sales. Another consideration is also involved here. Superior salesmen will not long remain with a company that ignores their claim to opportunity commensurate with their ability. Companies cannot afford to lose their best men to avoid upsetting less capable ones.

The best deserve the best. The meek might inherit the earth, but someone will have to take it in hand before giving it to his heirs. If the top producers don't receive the plums, disruption results and a sales force can be rent apart.

Rewarding the best seems a simple enough task, but actually it isn't as simple as it sounds. How do you define best? One man is outstanding in getting sales, another can conjure up new accounts seemingly out of thin air, a third hasn't lost an account or received a customer complaint in years, a fourth has personally trained a half dozen men who are now setting sales records in other parts of the country.

And territories: one is rich in profitable accounts, in another the sales potential will increase at a 15 per cent rate over the next ten years. Still another is experiencing a slow-but-steady economic erosion that will soon have a devastating effect on sales.

All this reinforces the statement that many factors must be analysed before a decision is made to reassign men to new territories.

Switching for Switching's Sake

Some authorities are so bold as to recommend a policy of periodic switching of men. They claim a new perspective, a new approach can be beneficial. A man too long on the same job loses his zest. He has trodden out his own rut and is content to remain within its confines.

A new man may be more amenable to direction if the switch is a step upward for him. He possibly will be more diligent in opening new accounts and doing missionary work. Complacent men, satisfied with what they are doing, will be shaken up, re-energized. New faces and approaches are necessary.

The opposing authorities are equally vehement. Stability and security are shaken by change, they state. Old relationships are broken. It is human nature to resist change and unreasoned change leads to unrest, loss of morale. Changing territories requires families to move, children to change schools — a traumatic experience for everyone involved in the process.

I feel it is important for us to dig into this switching business thoroughly. I have seen men ruined as a result of being switched to a new territory and I have seen others who destroyed themselves on a job who might have been saved had they been moved. Let's start by listing the pros and cons of random switching.

Change for the Sake of Change

Positive Results	Negative results
Perspective and attitude change in new environment	Sense of security is shaken
A new challenge should stimulate complacent men	Severing long-standing relationships destroys sense of belonging
New surroundings, new faces get a man out of a rut	Family life disrupted, roots are torn up
A transfer might cause a man to reassess his past performance and turn over a new leaf	Moves especially hard on children
	Morale often lowered
	The salesman is confused: 'What did I do wrong? Why am I being moved?'

Neither side is entirely right or wrong. Personally, I feel no change should be made based wholly on change for the sake of change. Changes should be made if a situation has deteriorated to a point that there is no hope of correcting it without a change and if there is a reasonable probability that the change will provide a successful solution to the problem.

Some changes will not be as unsettling as others. Moving a household from one location to another is expensive and harder for a family to handle emotionally than one that requires only that a man getting into his car in the morning head east instead of west. Such a change will primarily affect the man, but what upsets him upsets his whole family.

Only if a heavy preponderance of evidence favours the change should it be made. And remember, salesmen and their families are not draft animals, content as long as they receive a daily bag of oats.

A sales manager having serious problems with salesman A and considering shifting him to another territory might prepare a chart to help him decide what should be done. Suppose that numerous talks with the man in the past year have not resulted in noticeable improvement in his performance.

Salesman A

Problems	Effect of re-assignment
Sales less than satisfactory	Will start with a clean slate
Attitude not positive	Opportunity to leave behind negative attitude and get back to positive approach to job
Relations with customers in some cases strained	Chance to prove his ability in an atmosphere of his own making, away from past failure
Interest in job waning	Restored opportunity for advancement
Lack of attention to new accounts, missionary work, servicing accounts	
Complacent	
Behaviour might be influenced by poor choice of friends or unwise relationships formed.	

The sales manager is forced to conclude that if matters proceed in the present direction, the man will have to be terminated. He has been with the company for almost ten years and during much of that time has done better than an average job. His past service and his tenure with the company entitle him to consideration. He is a man worth saving and should be given another chance in a new location. If he succeeds all is well, if he fails again he must go.

The sales manager decides to make the switch in territory. He will call the salesman in, tell him why he is making the change and make him understand quite clearly that if his attitude and performance improve he is assured of holding his job. He must be aware that another failure will make it impossible for him to remain with the company.

I would approve such a transfer. It does not, of course, represent a switch for the sake of switching. There are many good reasons why the change should be made; I feel that equally good reasons should exist before *any* man is moved to another location.

Changes are unsettling. Too many can damage a sales force. Act only when action is necessary. Keep your salesmen abreast of company policy, let them know at all times how they are doing and what the future might have in store for them. Praise when praise is due, but when censure is required don't fail to deliver it. Finally, level with your men. Total honesty is not the best policy, it is the only policy when dealing with people.

Companies rock along on the momentum supplied by the hard-working average salesman, but expansion and growth come from the added impetus supplied by the top performers. To get the best out of his territory and his men a sales manager must be able to fit round pegs in round holes, square pegs in square holes. The more a sales manager knows about territories to be opened or reshuffled and the more he knows of the personality and qualities of his men, the better is the likelihood of making superior decisions on assignments.

Before going on to the next point let me stop a moment to make an observation. We have already talked about the experts who are pre-occupied with the conviction that the best salesman should always be encouraged to get promoted into higher prestige management jobs. Here again the word *best* raises its ugly head. The best salesman might be a chap who has an order book in his pocket and a full tank of petrol in his car. Start him off in the morning and he'll come back with a sheaf of orders. Would that man necessarily be the best at analysing the competition, territory potential and attainable market share? Would he possess all the other characteristics a sales manager should have? As the song tells us, it ain't necessarily so.

Using Commission Rates to Equalize Territories

Equalization of territories can be achieved by varying commission rates. Let us consider two territories.

Territory 1

Highly industrialized
Small, compact
Three major cities
High potential — 9 on scale of 10

Territory 2

Mainly rural
Large, spread out
Four widely separated cities
Low potential — 6 on scale of 10

The man covering territory 1 can be home every night. No account is more than an hour's drive from home.

The chap in territory 2 is not so fortunate. He must drive hundreds of miles each week, accounts are widely scattered, potential is not good and his expenses are high since he is away from home so many nights.

We all acknowledge that just as no two territories are similar, so also no two salesmen are similar. The man in territory 1 might be a top quality old-timer who earned the right to a good territory by paying his dues for years in territories like number 2. The man in territory 2 might be a new recruit starting to work his way up in the organization. No argument on this so far.

One school of thought might take the attitude 'so what, who says it's got to be fair? That's how the cookie crumbles. Take it or leave it.'

Yet, equity may suggest some commission differential in territory 2. The salesman might be required to pay his own expenses and commission rates could be increased to compensate. Expenses would then become a variable cost rather than fixed. The commission increase might be great enough to cover the salesman's expenses and leave something over for him. I am sure the company would not object, provided the salesman did the entertaining expected of him. That isn't a problem when company money is used, but the salesman might develop a latent sense of conservatism when spending his own money.

The company has an obligation to pay the salesman in territory 2 an adequate income, provided he does an acceptable job. What arrangement it makes is immaterial so long as the man is provided an opportunity to earn a living through his efforts.

Incidentally, surveys have indicated that older, more experienced commission-paid salesmen prefer to pay their own expenses and receive higher commission rates to compensate. Newer, less experienced men prefer that the commission rate be lower with the company being responsible for expenses.

Hints to Sales Managers

- Follow the seven steps when considering expansion into a new area.
- Optimism is great, but don't let your emotions colour your judgement.
- When opening a new territory, research the man you pick for the job as thoroughly as you analyse the area itself.
- When you cut a man's territory, particularly if he has done a good job for you in the past, he deserves consideration. Be sure he receives it.
- Remember that while a sales manager's primary responsiblity is to get sales for his company it is also of utmost importance that he be the ally of the salesmen in helping them to do the best job they can do for themselves.
- Re-assigning men to different territories may be necessary, but never move hastily, without carefully checking all factors involved.

Chapter 11

TARGETS

Targets can be set at all levels of a business. Quite often they start at the very top. The brass at the home office set the company objective for the year at sales of £100 million. It might as well be called a forecast as a target. A share of the total will be allocated to each division or region, broken down further until it reaches branch level. Every branch sales manager distributes his allotted total among his salesmen.

One major problem associated with this method of assigning targets down the line relates to the validity of the corporate sales objective. If the figure chosen is 20 per cent above the previous year's performance and there have been few changes in the overall situation that could affect gross volume favourably in the coming year, every target down to the amount assigned to a salesman might be 20 per cent above the ability to perform. On the other hand, an overall target set too low will provide little incentive for the various operating levels to function at full efficiency. In either event the company as a whole and each individual in the chain will suffer.

Another method of developing targets is to start at the other end, with the salesman. Branch managers set targets for their men. Totals are sent up the line through the management chain until they are finally consolidated by the company director of sales. How accurate the company objective will be if developed by this means will depend on the attitude and competence of the line managers who set the targets.

Some companies work it both ways. Targets filter down as others filter up. If totals roughly agree, all is well; if not, it's back to the drawing board for top and line management until mutually acceptable figures are arrived at.

Targets may be based on gross margin or profits instead of sales volume. Goals are set for regions, divisions and branches, and it is a sales manager's responsibility to establish targets for his men that will enable his office to meet its goal. Sophisticated accounting systems are necessary if each branch is to become a profit centre and sales managers must be able to convert profit back into gross sales or gross margin when allocating targets to individual salesmen. That isn't an easy assignment.

So much for where targets originate. For the moment we'll leave top management to its Olympian detachment and get in the trenches with branch sales managers. Why targets? What purpose do they serve? If targets are not well designed, they can be the bane of a sales manager's existence, the albatross chained to the neck of the salesman.

In ideal circumstances a target is an accurate measuring device to judge the performance of a salesman, a group of salesmen or an entire branch. Also, if properly prepared and used, it can be a powerful stimulant to every member of a sales force. Perforce, a target should be equitable, realistic and at least approximately attainable by conscientious and intelligent effort. It should encourage the individual or group for which it is set to achieve adequate or, preferably, superior performance.

Targets also serve as an integral factor in determining a salesman's earnings. Generally, sales above target command a higher commission rate or entitle the salesman to a bonus. Many plans even start the extra compensation at 85 per cent or 90 per cent of target and the rate of extra compensation increases as plateaus above target are reached.

Only with regressive commisson plans do rates drop once target has been achieved. Targets should stimulate a man to do his job better, not punish him for superior performance.

If targets are set too high, the stimulating effect is lost. Who can get charged up about an unobtainable goal? Organizations that impose unreasonable targets on a sales force and then pressure the men to meet them achieve only negative reactions on the part of the men, overselling and, consequently, damaged customer relations.

Targets can point salesmen's efforts in directions deemed important to the company. For example, if a company feels it necessary to add new customers it will stimulate a salesman in this area if a goal is set for him and a bonus paid to attain it.

A target is a useful device by which a sales manager can measure the relative performance of his men. Targets will vary among men, but each man's target should reflect the manager's perception of what he is capable of accomplishing, given his innate ability and the potential in his territory. If all targets are set equitably, the manager has a built-in method of establishing the relative performance of each of his men by comparing the percentages of targets reached.

One thing a target will not do. It can indicate which men have done well and which have done poorly, but it cannot answer the question why each man performed as he did. For the answer to that, the sales manager must rely on his knowledge of the personal strengths and weaknesses of his men.

Are disadvantages connected with the use of a target? Some people say there are. They claim that targets are highly subjective in creation and are an inaccurate base for establishing goals. The result of a poor target can be damage to a sales force. They are right but only if the target set is inaccurate. Good sales managers set accurate and realistic targets.

Another complaint is that installing and operating with a target system puts a heavy load of work on a sales manager. So what? Sales managers are paid to work.

The third complaint is that targets impose high pressure on salesmen to the detriment of their performance. I don't buy this either. No man can work efficiently and effectively if he is not aware of what is expected of him. If his target has been set fairly and is realistically attainable, I see no reason for him to feel overpressured. Again, it is up to the sales manager to get the targets right. If he can't, it's time to get someone on the job who can.

One last point before we talk about setting up a target system. Targets will be effective aids in supplying incentive to men, especially when a substantial part of their compensation stems from commission. When a bonus is the prize for attainment of a target it provides an even greater stimulant. I won't go into the argument whether a sense of achievement or material reward is the most powerful motivator. Give a man opportunity to gain both and you can't lose.

To be effective targets must be understood and accepted by salesmen. Acceptance is of vital importance; a man won't work for something he doesn't believe in. Wise managers will go over each man's target with him, making sure he understands it and realizes what attainment of it can mean to him.

Four bases are commonly used in setting up a target system at the branch level. Discussion of each follows.

Anticipated Volume of Sales

The sales manager estimates the volume of sales expected, basing his estimate on an analysis of the market situation as it presently obtains. In doing this he takes steps similar to those taken when evaluating the potential in a territory. Among the factors he studies are:

1. The total market in the territory or district.
2. The competitive position of his company.
3. The presently projected share of market that can be obtained.
4. The quality of the coverage of the market. This, of course, depends on a subjective judgement of the ability of the men covering the area.
5. Past performance in the area. Historical data should be adjusted to conform with changes to be made in personnel, territories or company policies. The effect of new products to be introduced, price adjustments and even expected economic conditions should also be built into the estimate.

From this analysis sales forecasts are made for individuals and for the branch.

Gross Margin and Cost of Sale

These elements are introduced in order to ensure that excessive emphasis will not be placed on gross sales revenue to the detriment of financial considerations. Under this approach, adjusted gross margin on unit sales instead of sales revenue is used as a base for establishing a target. A careful analysis of the gross margin of company products will be made and the target will be further adjusted through the deduction of cost of sale, which in this case does not include salesmen's compensation. This is how the computation sets up:

Gross sales	£300,000
Cost of goods sold	210,000
Gross margin	90,000
Cost of sale	10,000
Adjusted gross margin	80,000

Refer back to Chapter 4 for an explanation of the method of handling gross margin used as a base for paying commission. Remember not to include salesmen's compensation in the cost of sale.

In setting up a target based on adjusted gross margin care should be exercised that the multiplier effect is not ignored. Which would you rather have, sales of £100,000 with margin of £20,000 or £75,000 with a margin of £25,000? Perhaps the addition of £25,000 of overhead absorbing gross sales may be more important than £5,000 gross margin. The question isn't always a simple one to answer.

Sales managers have to think as well as act; a good portion of their earnings may stem from the profitability of their branches. So, if you use this type of target be sure you get it right.

Normal Non-selling Activities

Another frequently used base for a target system is a measure of other than direct selling activities of a salesman. These may consist of:

1. Merchandising responsibilities
2. Demonstrations
3. Soliciting new accounts, reactivating closed ones
4. Setting up displays and other promotional work

5. Service and customer calls for help or advice
6. Training new men

None of these activities result in an immediate pay-off either to the company or to the salesman. Yet, the effort must be expended if the territory is to achieve its full potential. Unfortunately, the performance of these functions must be rated on a largely subjective basis by the sales manager. He can, of course, study a salesman's reports for a basic count of time spent and calls made, but he must rely on his judgement to estimate the future value of the salesman's efforts in these peripheral activities.

It would be a most unusual situation indeed if these factors were of sufficient importance that the target for a man was based entirely on them, but an appraisal of performance on these duties could be given a weight in determining his overall target.

Combination Targets

Using more than a single factor on which to base a target will provide a solid foundation for goal setting. The broader and the more accurately computed it is the greater is the probability of setting realistic projections for the salesman and the company to achieve. Formulation of such plans is complex, much more complicated than setting a gross sales goal, but the results can amply repay the additional effort required to set them up.

Some facets can be given a priority rating if the weighting scheme is based on the relative importance of each element. The chart constructed here will illustrate how a combination target might be set up. This salesman achieved 96.5 per cent of target.

	Weight	*Target*	*Performance*	*Per cent of target*	*Times weight*
Sales	45	£400,000	£440,000	110%	4,950
Gross margin	25	£100,0000	£ 80,000	80%	2,000
New accounts	20	40	30	75%	1,500
Service, training, etc	10	60	72	120%	1,200
	100				9,650

The example placed primary emphasis on sales volume (45 per cent weight), followed by a target gross margin of 25 per cent (25 per cent weight). New accounts followed just behind (20 per cent weight) and the balance of the target is based on service, training and so forth. The company should meet its objectives in each area if targets are met. Indeed, targets may have been set so that 90 per cent performance is the realistic goal for the salesmen and the company to reach.

Let us take a closer look at the performance of the man whose record is reported. He is obviously a good salesman, but like many men of his calibre he has apparently been concentrating on selling high-volume low-margin products. You will note he sold 110 per cent of sales volume target, but achieved only 80 per cent of gross margin target. He excels in the service and training areas, possibly at the expense of soliciting new accounts.

The chart contains much information useful to a sales manager when he discusses performance with a salesman. Computing performance using a chart like the example is purely a mathematical exercise except in the final category where the sales manager will have to rely on his personal knowledge of the salesman and an analysis of his reports.

Naturally each company wil have to choose the elements to be included in a combined target system and apply weights that relate to the importance of each company objective.

Targets

From salesman's viewpoint	From company's viewpoint
Let men know what is expected of them	Provide a tool to measure and compare performance of men
Provide incentive for attainment	Can direct salesmen's attention to areas important to company
Provide bonuses for superior performance	If poorly designed, can have damaging influence on morale and performance of men
If set too high, will discourage men, pressure them	Are a useful factor in setting compensation plans for men
If set too low, will cheapen sense of attainment	

Hints to Sales Managers

- Targets should set realistic goals for salesmen, not impose an unbearable burden on them.
- Targets should stimulate, not depress.
- To assign effective targets, you must first know the capability of your men, the level of performance that can be expected of them.
- Go over his target with each of your men. Make sure he understands what is expected of him and what he can earn if he reaches his goal.
- Combination targets are hard to develop and administer, but may improve performance markedly. Be aware of the benefits that can accrue from them.

Chapter 12

POLICY DECISIONS

Special situations are always arising with respect to rewarding salesmen when a company does a substantial volume of business. We'll go into several types of transactions that require special handling, but before we do so, we'll write a few words about general company policy on the occasions when a salesmen's reward scheme is affected.

Equity is involved, of course — equity for the salesman and the company. So is realism. Some things are possible, others aren't. To insure a good relationship between a salesman and his employer each must trust and respect the other. Each must believe there is a good reason for whatever is done, a reason that makes sense. Salesmen have rights, as do companies. Judgements should never be hasty or ill-advised, they should be well thought through before they are announced.

When policies are established, the sales force should receive a full explanation so the reason for the policy is understood as well as its application. There will be no acceptance on the part of the salesman without understanding. When that fact is ignored, as it often is, unrest and complaints are generated with the result that both sides suffer.

When Is a Sale a Sale?

There are at least three answers to that question and from the point of view of some salesmen it makes a great deal of difference which is chosen. The three options are:

1. When the order is received.
2. When the order is despatched and invoiced.
3. When the payment is received.

We are interested only in what effect each choice will have on a salesman. Company accounting practices are a different matter and we will not concern ourselves with them.

A salesman paid a straight salary is not overly concerned at what point the company decides a sale has been made, but a commission man and one who derives part of his reward from a bonus have a substantial stake in the decision. Such a person would like to receive his commission and credit for a sale when he turns in the order. The company might feel there's many a slip between cup and lip. It would prefer to pay commission at the time the order is shipped and invoiced. The interval between receipt of order and delivery could be weeks or even months.

Other companies are even more conservative paying the salesman only when payment has been received from the customer. In general, companies adopting this policy are concerned with the credit standing of their customers or the possibility of cancellation of the order. Companies selling to customers of impeccable financial standing should have no qualms about paying a salesman when an order is shipped and billed, or perhaps even when the order is received.

It isn't only the commission that concerns the salesman. If he is paid on a commission plus bonus plan, he might need the sales revenue to meet his quota in a period. Any delay in crediting the sale to his account may result in lower earnings for him.

Except in those cases where a long time elapses between the receipt of an order and its delivery, the policy of considering a sale made when goods are shipped and invoiced appears to be a good one. Changes in quantities and prices will already have been made and commission expense will be offset against receipt of payment for the goods. When an appreciable time passes before goods are shipped, a partial payment of commission can be made on receipt of the order with the balance due at time of invoice.

Only in cases where there is a serious doubt whether payment will be made or there is a real possibility that the order may be cancelled before goods are delivered is there a valid reason for holding commission until the invoice is honoured.

As we have said, it is largely immaterial to worry about when a sale becomes a sale if the sales force is rewarded entirely by salary. It does become important when commission and bonuses are involved. Companies should establish a firm, clear policy on the subject and make sure the sales force understands the policy fully.

Instalment Sales

How does a company pay a commission on a £1,000 sale when the customer pays £200 down and the balance over the next 18 months? In some cases full commission is paid at once, in others only a percentage of it is considered earned when the sale is made and additional amounts are paid as instalments are received. The amount of commission paid up front depends on the size of the down payment.

It is difficult to set up controls under this method of payment. Administrative costs are high. Expensive, yes, but customers have been known to renege on their obligations and even disappear with the merchandise. That costs the company even more, especially when full commission has been paid. In such an event a policy should be established to cover the repayment of a portion or all of the commission paid before default. Further adjustment can be made depending on whether or not the merchandise was recovered.

One further comment: in some industries, such as house-to-house selling of appliances, where customer failure to meet contractual obligations is an unfortunate fact of life, payment of commission as contract payments are received can serve two additional purposes. The salesman will be more interested in assisting collection efforts if he has a stake in the money collected. Also, commission receivable on a number of still-open contracts that make payments on schedule can be a strong influence to hold a man on the job since, should he quit, he would forfeit the remaining balance of commission.

Bad Debts

What happens when a salesman sells a carload of gravel to a road contractor who spreads it over ten miles of country dirt roads and then becomes insolvent before making payment? In this example the problem is compounded since there is no possibility of recovering the material.

The first question to be asked is: Who approved credit? If the salesman was authorized to pass on the credit worthiness of his customers, the company would appear to have the right to say that since no money was received, no sale took place and no commission would be payable. I should hope that if a second disaster of this type occurred, the sales manager would have a few words to say to the salesman.

On the other hand, suppose the salesman submitted the order to the office, which according to company policy passed on all credit, and the office approved the sale. The salesman would seem to have at least some claim to commission. He did his job: if the office goofed, let it pay for its mistake.

These are tricky situations. Whatever policy a company adopts to cover them, it should be clearly stated and understood by the salesmen.

Returns

Goods are returned for many reasons. Among them are:

1. Shoddy workmanship, failure to meet specifications
2. Late delivery
3. Overselling or misrepresentation by the salesman
4. Change in manufacturing requirements by the customer

No hard and fast rules can be established to fix responsibility for every return. An investigation should be made, the reason for the return established as accurately as possible and the party at fault identified. If the company was at fault, the salesman should not be penalized. If he made the mistake, he should reap no benefit from his action. If neither the company nor the salesman was to blame, a suitable settlement should be made with the salesman.

Should an old and valued customer return goods for full credit because of a change in manufacturing process or product, the company could, as a matter of good customer relations, accept the return and allow the salesman to retain all or part of this commission. Yet, some companies have a firm policy of paying commission only when delivery is made and payment received. Again, let the company express its policy clearly and make sure everyone understands it.

Long-Term Sales

On occasion a salesman might be fortunate enough to secure an order covering the sale of goods extending for a period of months or even years. If he is a salaried man, no problems exist. If the order runs to a lot of money, he is reasonably assured he will be given a rise and that is the end of the matter. If he should be paid on a commission base, with or without a bonus arrangement, the problem of the timing of his pay becomes complicated.

Let us set up a transaction and see how we can handle it. We will assume a salesman receives an order for a ton of a certain material to be delivered each month for a period of five years. The present price of the product is £6,000 a ton and the contract ties future prices to an agreed upon commodity index. There is a provision in the contract that it can be cancelled by the purchaser at the end of the third or fourth year, provided a penalty of the value of one ton of the product at the then-current price is paid to the company. Let us also assume the salesman is paid a 3 per cent commission and receives a bonus if he meets an annual target of sales revenue. Incidentally, it took the salesman nearly a year to secure the order.

The question is: When should commission be paid to the salesman and in what annual periods should sales be credited against his target? For the sake of simplicity we'll assume the price holds steady at £6,000 a ton. The transaction sets up like this:

One ton per month at £6,000 per ton	£72,000	per year
Length of contract	× 5	years
Total value of contract	£360,000	
Commission	× 3	per cent
Total commission payable	£ 10,800	

To pay the entire commission to the salesman when the first ton is shipped and add the whole £360,000 to his sales production at that time would be unreasonable. After all, the order might be cancelled at the end of three or four years by payment of a £6,000 penalty.

Yet, for three years the contract is firm. In that period sales would total £216,000 (£6,000 a month for 36 months). Commission at 3 per cent would amount to £6,480. Suppose the salesman is paid ⅓ of the commission when the first ton is shipped and the remaining ⅔ in monthly instalments as the goods are shipped. This is how it would work out.

Sales of £6,000 a month for 36 months	£216,000
Commission at 3 per cent	6,480
⅓ paid when first shipment is made	2,160
Balance of commission	£ 4,320
Payments per month for 36 months	£ 120

If the contract were cancelled at the end of year 3, the salesman would be paid £180 commission on the penalty payment received. If the contract remained in force, he would receive £180 a month for the fourth year, and again in the fifth year if the contract ran its full course.

Credit against his target could be handled in the same fashion. That is, he would receive credit for ⅓ of the total three-year turnover (£72,000) at the time the first delivery was made and an additional £48,000 for each of the first three years. In the final two years of the contract he would receive credit for £72,000 sales a year.

That would appear an equitable method of handling the situation. The five year annuity feature would appeal to the salesman, as would the substantial initial payment. The company would find the plan attractive: substantial front money for the salesman and further commission paid over the life of the contract. That feature might be an important incentive for the salesman to continue in the employ of the company.

The company could not be faulted for being reluctant to pay full commission on contracted sales for three years at the time of the first delivery. After all, no contract is ironclad; companies go out of business. Basically, it is prudent to relate commission payments and bonuses as closely as possible to actual delivery of goods.

I am not offering this solution to the problem of paying commission on long-term sales as a panacea. Each company will adopt a policy suited to its situation. The suggestion is offered for the purpose of spurring each company toward finding the solution that suits it and its salesmen best.

House Accounts

Rule I — Limit as rigidly as possible

Rule II — Clearly define what accounts will be included in the category.

Many accounts can legitimately be classified as house accounts. For instance, the owner of an auto distributorship personally makes a deal with a local auto rental company for a number of cars to be delivered each year. Credit for such a sale correctly belongs to the agency.

On the other hand, suppose a salesman has been selling a company regularly and receiving steady, medium-sized orders from it. One day the sales manager receives a call from the purchasing department for an order of substantial size. In my estimation, to designate such an order as belonging to the office is a serious mistake. It was the salesman's account. He built a relationship with the company and provided needed service to it. The sale is rightfully his.

An argument could also be made that a salesman would be entitled to commission if he had consistently been calling on the company and had not, up to the present, been able to sell it. The order, even if called in to the office, should be his.

In general, house accounts are large ones and are developed by the sales manager or the home office. They often require special handling, and price concessions because of volume are not unusual.

No salesman should be denied financial reward if he develops a customer, even though the size and complexity of an order is beyond his authority or his ability to resolve. It might be necessary to involve the sales manager, a home-office executive and factory engineers in the deal, but the salesman started it all and it is his sale. After all, aren't sales managers, executives and engineers paid to do their jobs and lend assistance where needed? Circumstances should dictate whether or not the salesman should receive full commission.

Time may be an ally when resolving some sticky situations. Let us say that a salesman has developed in his territory one extremely lucrative account, the handling of which is so complex that management is frequently called on for assistance. The salesman has made a handsome income from the account and when he retires the territory is assigned to another man. It is a rich territory even without the one large account. Under the circumstances management might transfer the customer to house-account status. There can be little argument with the decision, provided an arrangement is made to reward the person who is assigned to service the account. The same action might be taken if territories are redefined and men reassigned.

If a branch has a large number of house accounts, it would not be surprising to find a degree of unrest in the sales force. An excessive number would indicate that the company should re-examine its policy on house accounts. When the only objective of classifying an account as a house account is to avoid paying commission, the company will deserve the consequences of its act.

Split Commissions

Another problem causer. Split commissions only when truly necessary. I can think of two circumstances under which splitting is justified.

A salesman calls on the central buying office of a corporation in Bristol and secures a contract for a piece of equipment to be installed in a plant in Leeds. He is entitled to be compensated for his effort, but so is the Leeds salesman who must install the machinery and train its operator.

In another case a salesman makes a contact and secures the opportunity to bid on a job. The sales manager is called on to make the bid and he enlists the aid of factory engineers in modifying standard equipment to meet special specifications. Factory technicians will install the machinery when delivered. The originating salesman is the only one of the whole group paid on commission, and he certainly has earned some share of the commission for originating the sale. How much he receives depends on the value of his contribution.

Splitting commission may be the only answer when more than one man and one territory are involved in a sale. When such circumstances are frequent, a company should establish a clear and well-understood policy to handle them.

Unsolicited Telephone and Mail Orders

Many companies encourage small accounts to order by these methods. Not infrequently, inquiries come from out-of-the-way places and often it is not economic for a salesman to schedule regular calls on such customers.

I see no reason not to pay the territory salesman full commission on these sales. Who knows — a follow-up call might result in additional sales. To call these found sales house accounts is a contemptible display of parsimony.

Commission Pools

Many sales managers throw extra commissions into a pool to be distributed among salesmen. These monies can come from several sources.

In some cases territories are not rigidly defined and several men work in an area. Should a customer not previously called on or sold call in an order, the commission would properly be thrown into the pool.

A sales manager who picks up a modest order on the golf course on Saturday afternoon might contribute the commission to the pool before assigning the account to one of his men. A split commission share might have been received from another office and the sales manager himself handled the installation and follow-up. That commission, too, might be added to the pool provided the sales manager was thinking more of his men than himself. Bits and pieces of commission come from a surprising variety of sources.

Some enlightened sales managers consistently allocate a portion of the commission not actually paid on house accounts to the pot. To me, this is a smart practice. It is a relatively inexpensive way to provide money for a prize fund. If the fund stimulates salesmen to better performance the results can be most rewarding.

The pool should be distributed according to an established plan at regular intervals or when the pool reaches a predetermined amount. It can be:

1. Equally divided among the men. I don't like this method of distribution. A man should earn everything he gets.
2. Raffled off. I don't care for this either. Prizes should be used as incentives. Reward the person or persons who respond best to a challenge.
3. Offered as a prize, or prizes if the pool is large enough, for winners of a contest. Base the contest on whatever you will: the number of new accounts opened in a specific period, sales of a new product the company is pushing, etc.

A contest adds zest. Salesmen respond to a challenge. Even if the prize isn't all that valuable, it appeals to the competitive spirit of a salesman.

Trade-ins

Every company has its own policy on handling trade-ins. It also varies from industry to industry. Many companies pay commission based on sales less allowances. This is particularly common when the traded in merchandise is of little worth and is sold for scrap value. In other cases, such as in the automobile business, the trade-in has a substantial worth. Some salesmen are given the responsibility of disposing of trade-ins they accept; in other cases a different sales force is employed for the purpose. Some trade-ins are sold as is, others receive varying amounts of restoration before resale.

Trade-in policies don't just grow, they become established after long and sometimes expensive trial and error. My advice to a company is to adopt the same basic policy that prevails in the industry and not to fool around too much with innovations.

Windfalls

We have left a discussion of this topic for last, and for a very good reason. You may already have inferred from my earlier statements on 'excessive' earnings of salesmen and regressive commission plans that I am not in favour of curtailing earnings of salesmen as a matter of policy.

In general, the same thinking colours my attitude toward windfalls. Let us look at three types of orders that can be considered as windfalls.

In the first, a salesman calling on a regular customer secures an unexpected one-time gigantic order, the commission on which in the normal course of events would amount to £20,000.

Sales management literature is encyclopedic on the subject of how such a transaction should be handled. The majority of experts agree that the salesman should not reap the benefit of his unexpected bonanza. They are the same individuals who favour regressive commission plans as a tool to hold down salesmen's earnings. There are valid arguments in favour of regressive schedules under some circumstances and even of preventing certain types of huge windfall payments. I can, however, accept no argument that would deprive a salesman of his commission in this case.

Attempts are made to persuade us that since the salesman expended little or no special effort or had little influence in securing the order, he is not entitled to the commission. If effort is the criterion for paying a man, why doesn't a company reward a salesman for the hours or days he spends in a vain effort to sell a customer? The buyer was the salesman's customer. He got the order fair and square.

There is no valid reason, ethical or otherwise, why the salesman should not receive his commission. To make such a sale a house account and pay no commission simply transfers the windfall to the company, which did nothing to create the sale.

The experts even object to payment on windfall sales because of the old argument that such payments might result in a salesman being paid more than his boss. This, they say, would reduce the sales manager's authority and devalue the prospect of promotion to management. I have already addressed this fallacy and will not go into it again.

We are also told that paying a windfall commission is grossly unfair to other men. How is this, we ask? I'm not sure of the answer, but it seems to come down to the assumption that a person is not entitled to such a lucky break that is not available to every other man.

To the contrary, I should think the response of the rest of the sales force would be, 'Joe sure hit the jackpot, lucky stiff. Maybe it'll happen to me next time'. I *know* what the reaction of the other men would be if Joe were denied the commission: 'Cheap chiselers. Why should I break my back working for this company when if I get a lucky break they'll cheat me out of the commission?'

Another proponent of the restrictive policy fears that the sudden spurt in earnings might have a negative effect on a man, obligating him for greater and unplanned tax liability. It might even cause the unfortunate chap foolishly to expect a continuing stream of windfalls, causing him to start living above his means. Thus, for his own good it is better to keep a man earning at his regular pace and be sure you don't complicate his life by paying him more than he is accustomed to. I will make no comment on these suggestions.

In some cases a so-called windfall may be accompanied by a request for a price concession. Terms and prices would be worked out by company executives and if a discount were allowed, the salesman should be willing to bear his fair share of the concession through a reduced rate of commission. Notice, I said *fair*.

A final word on this type of windfall: For the mutual advantage of the company and the salesman there must be mutual respect and trust. Destroy either element and irreparable damage will inevitably be done to both parties.

Our second example is substantially different. A salesman calling on an established account is given his normal order and is then informed that a new policy of centralized buying has been adopted under which his customer will purchase all the requirements for five other factories in different areas of the country.

The salesman should continue to be paid commission on all sales to the customer for consumption in the local plant, but there is no reason to compensate him for orders originating in far places and passing through the local factory merely for the convenience of the customer. The salesmen who covered those distant plants have a much more valid claim to the commission. They still call on the customer, service the account and, except for the change in policy, would continue to book the orders covering the plant's needs.

Should the other plants not have been customers, sales to them could rightly be considered house accounts. The men asked to service these new locations should be rewarded for their time. Undoubtedly they will rue the fact that they failed to make the plant a customer.

The third example is still different. The sales director in London meets the purchasing director of a company with which little business has been done in the past. After golf at the club they hammer out a deal over a couple of drinks that will result in sales of above £1 million for a line of products never before sold to that company.

Such an account should properly be considered a house account and a home-office one to boot. The district in which the merchandise is delivered has no valid claim to include the sale in its volume when bonuses for exceeding target are computed. Again, the man who services the account should be rewarded for his efforts.

The cardinal rule on windfalls: be ethical, be equitable. Don't toss your money around indiscriminately, but always pay a man what he has earned.

One personal note before we leave windfalls. Many years ago the accountant of a firm that bought and sold paper in bulk to printers and publishers approached the president of the company. He said that friends of his, a couple, were starting publication of a new type of magazine and wished to place an order for paper. Finances were tight for them, the accountant said, but he was positive the couple would honour their obligation for the paper. The owner trusted the judgement of his financial man and authorized delivery of the paper, adding that as the accountant had originated the sale he would be entitled to a salesman's commission.

The magazine flourished. Its circulation multiplied astronomically into the millions. Not too long afterward the accountant retired to a life of leisure. A windfall? Perhaps, but who was hurt when the commission was paid? A delightful story, and true too. Everyone was better off because it happened.

Hints to Sales Managers

- Be ready for problems before they arise. Do your thinking ahead of time.
- Know every detail of company policy that can affect your men.
- Share your knowledge with them.
- 'Why?' How often have you heard that despairing query? A decision is more likely to be accepted if the salesman knows the rule on which it is based.
- Avoid surprises. Bolts from the blue are viewed with cynicism.
- Remember you are the middle-man between the company and your men. You represent them both. Each has rights. Make sure they secure them.

Chapter 13

DEVELOPING A TOTAL REWARD SCHEME

We've come a long way down the road together and it's nearly time for us to construct a reward scheme from the elements we have been discussing. First, however, we should consider a few basic factors that will, to a large extent, control the design of the plan that will best fit your company. While we do all this, don't lose sight of the three basic objectives of a reward scheme. They are:

1. To pay an employee for his services in such a way that reward is commensurate with contribution.
2. To provide incentive for the salesman to strive constantly to do ever better for himself.
3. To design the plan so that it will be a positive force in helping the company to achieve its sales goals.

Keep those three statements firmly in mind while we run through the factors that will influence your choice of a total reward scheme.

Financial Considerations

The company must survive while it is building a sales force or entering a new market. If cash is a scarce commodity, the company will not be able to pay its sales force a substantial salary and must rely mainly on commission representatives. On the other hand, when a new division of a multi-million pound corporation organizes a sales force, its plan will be based on what is best rather than what is expedient. Few companies should experience difficulty in deciding into which category they fit.

Nature of Market and Method of Distribution

There appear to be generally accepted practices in reward schemes of a number of industries. For example, house-to-house salesmen for products such as vacuum cleaners, cosmetics and kitchenware are usually paid commission only. There are sound reasons for this.

At the other end of the spectrum are the highly educated, highly trained men selling expensive and complicated machinery or high-tech products. Such individuals generally receive a substantial salary as the major portion of their pay packages.

Whether a man is expected to call on 15 wholesalers or 150 retail establishments should also influence a reward scheme.

A company entering a new field should make a thorough study of the reward schemes of established companies already in the business. If the reward schemes of the competitors follow a similar pattern, it probably would not be wise for the newcomer to attempt to blaze a trail of his own. Experience will have influenced the others and one can profit as much from the experience of others as from one's own.

Nature of the Salesman's Job

What is the relative importance of the various elements of the work expected of a salesman? We have analysed possible job responsibilities in earlier sections of the book. Among them, some are better rewarded by salary, others by commission. What is important here is to understand what the company is looking for and choose the most effective way to pay for it.

Rewarding New Men

It probably would not be desirable to put inexperienced recruits just starting in a business on the same scheme that is used for a veteran sales force, especially if it relies heavily on commission rewards. A starter scheme might be designed to carry a new man through the training process until he could be expected to carry his own weight in the organization. Such a scheme might start with straight salary, and in a transition stage substitute a drawing account for salary until commission earnings could build to a suitable level.

Sales Force Profile

A company must be aware of the calibre of people it presently employs or intends to hire. Salespeople come in a multitude of shapes and sizes. They vary in age, sex, in temperament, education and background, in intellectual capacity. They have diferent aspirations. Some have an excellent idea how to fulfil them, others float with the current, seemingly unaware or even unconcerned where it is carrying them.

No company can construct a perfect profile of the ideal representative and hire only those who conform to the model. After all, how important is the difference between a *B* and a *B*– average in school or college?

Nevertheless, there are differences between individuals of similar age or background. One may earn £15,000 to £20,000 a year while the other makes three or four times as much.

Don't make a mistake when defining difference by assuming the higher earner is the better man. He might be, but there is no assurance that he is. There is a place for both men in our scheme of things. Any person, regardless of his economic status, is a credit to himself and to society in general if he is applying himself to his work to the best of his ability.

What Level of Earnings Should be Targeted

Having completed our preliminary analysis, let's get down to work. The earnings-level target figure selected will be controlled to a considerable extent by competitive influences. Certain industries historically pay more or less than others. Textile and apparel salesmen are usually near the top of the scale, lumber and building material salesmen much lower.

The government and many private research organisations issue comprehensive statistical information on industry-average compensation of salesmen. Even though the material may already be a year or two old when published, it is highly indicative of industry standards and trends.

Any reward scheme should be in line with those of the competition. Markedly excessive pay for similar work, while attracting the best quality representatives, would be counter-productive if it resulted in uncompetitive prices or loss of profits. Conversely, an appreciably lower scale would make it difficult to hire qualified men and at the same time result in the loss of experienced agents.

Designing a Scheme

Let us look at an example of how a reward scheme might be set up. First, a realistic profile for earnings of a prototype salesman will be established. We will pick £30,000 as a starter; it may be too high or too low, but it will do as an example. Furthermore, it is a good round figure that simplifies the mathematics.

We will assume that the company in question has decided to pay its sales force a mixture of salary, commission and bonus. Further analysis has resulted in the establishment of values for the various functions the salesmen are expected to perform and has indicated the type of compensation to be paid for each activity. That may sound complicated, but study of the chart should clarify the explanation.

Job requirements	*Salary*	*Commission*	*Bonus*	*Total weight*
Training new men	10		5	15
New accounts	5		5	10
Merchandising, promotion, servicing	10			10
Sales — adjusted gross margin	30	30	5	65
	55	30	15	100

We can see that the selling function is by far the most heavily weighted (65 of 100 total points). We also note that more than half of the points (55) are allocated to salary, 30 to commission and the balance to bonus. Since the target earnings figure is £30,000, each point would represent £300 in compensation. Thus, if a salesman hit every facet of the job on the nose he would earn exactly £30,000, broken down as follows:

Salary (55 × £300)	=	£16,500
Commission (30 × £300)	=	9,000
Bonus (15 × £300)	=	4,500
Total		£30,000

Observe — everything is in balance. How wonderful if only 10 per cent of salesmen were.

Analysis of Scheme

We'll start our discussion with the thinking of the company as it developed the scheme. A number of factors come to light.

The company considers as most important the selling activities of its salesmen. Sixty-five points of 100 are allocated to this function — 65 per cent, if you prefer.

Traning new men is an important facet of a salesman's job — 15 per cent. Opening new accounts and general promotional work account for the balance of a man's responsibility.

When we look at the three components of compensation — salary, commission and bonus, we observe that the company expects that salary will represent 55 per cent of total compensation. This indicates first that the sales force is expected to be composed of well-motivated, high-calibre individuals and also that the company is in a stable financial condition. Such a heavy concentration in the salary area will give the company a high degree of control over its agents.

Almost half the salary will be paid for training, opening new accounts and doing service and promotional work. The sales force is expected to earn bonus points for working with new men and adding new customers. The company is doing all it can to emphasize the importance of good performance in these areas.

You will notice that almost half of a salesman's reward for selling is paid by salary, the remainder by commission and bonus. The high share of salary should give the salesman a sense of stability and security in earnings while the commission segment is sufficiently large to motivate him.

It is also evident that the company is putting emphasis on the sale of products with higher gross margin rather than on gross volume of sales.

Note: One curious fact comes to light as we study the chart. A salesman meeting his sales target will receive a bonus equivalent to 5 per cent of his projected earnings. He can earn bonuses of similar amounts by meeting the performance objectives set for him in training new men and opening new accounts. Ordinarily we would expect to see exceptional achievement in sales production rewarded generously. It is possible, of course, that the 5 per cent bonus would increase should the salesman exceed his target. To me that is a reasonable conjecture.

It is also quite possible that this particular company is in a period of planned growth and expansion. Thus, trained new salesmen and an increase in its customer base are essential. I get the feeling that this company knows what it is doing and why it is doing it.

Targets under the Scheme

At this point we have formulated a basic scheme, chosen the methods of rewarding each of the salesman's functions and established a scale of values for rating their importance. Now it is time for us to set up a target system for each of the salesman's responsibilities, a mark for him to attain. Targets will be established so that if the salesman meets them he will have reached the earnings objective set for him and the company will have achieved its own goals.

It is in setting these targets and explaining them to his men that a sales manager earns a good portion of his keep. In one territory the resident salesman has no knack for or interest in training new men. It would be useless to attempt to force him to do his share of training. He would turn new men off rather than on. Thus, the sales manager would transfer the points allocated to this function to another area where the salesman could be expected to improve his performance.

What I am saying is that the sales manager must be prepared to hand-tailor the scheme to the capabilities and characteristics of his men. The better the job he does, the higher are the prospects of drawing the best from each member of the sales force.

Hand-tailored suits fit better than ready-made ones. The sales manager's job is to work with the demonstrated strengths of his men, rely on the abilities they have displayed and at the same time attempt to develop new strengths in men who have evidenced a willingness to learn and grow.

Of course, the size of an organization has a great effect on the amount of hand-fitting a sales manager can do. With a force of a dozen or so men he can fit a scheme to each man. Should he have 50 or more salesmen under his control, hand-tailoring would be almost out of the question. Yet, the sales manager need not despair; men can be divided into classes and different requirements set for each class. More on this later.

Training New Men

We might presume that the company is attempting to expand and needs to add to its sales force. As a consequence, experienced salesmen who have $ bent for this type of work are expected to take a number of new recruits in the field with them for specified periods of time. The trainer is paid for this work and would also be entitled to a bonus for at least meeting his training responsibilities.

New Accounts

A target would be set for each salesman, depending on what results the sales manager can reasonably expect from the territory. He will be influenced by territorial potential, by the experience and ability of the individual men and by any other relevant factors. A bonus would be paid if the target were met or exceeded.

Miscellaneous Promotional Work

The only way a sales manager can monitor activity and performance would be through personal observation and study of reports filed by his men. Not an easy task, but remember, more than half a salesman's reward derives from salary. This fact gives the sales manager the authority and right to control the activities of his men.

How well a salesman discharges his responsibility in this area will be a matter of personal judgement of the sales manager. The better he knows his men, the more accurate will be his assessment of the job done.

Sales

The target will be developed in line with the principles covered in an earlier chapter of this book. It will be based on gross sales volume less cost of goods sold less the cost of sale other than salesman's rewards (adjusted gross margin).

When a target has been established, the sales manager will check the cost of sale including expected rewards of £30,000 against the gross volume of sales. If total cost of sale as a percentage of gross sales are within the company established guideline, all is well. If not, it is back to the drawing board for the sales manager. Either the salesman isn't being asked for enough production or he is being over-paid by company standards.

Perhaps the salesman could be a mite free with the company money he throws around when entertaining customers. The sales manager checks this possibility and may have a few words with the offender. Never forget, even though a man is paid for accomplishing a number of duties, the money to pay for them must be supplied by the proceeds of what he sells. The company has no other source of income.

Let us now put some numbers on our example. Assume a gross sales target of £450,000. Average adjusted gross margin for the company is 28 per cent. Adjusted gross margin on £450,000 is £126,000. Since the salesman is expected to earn £9,000 commission for selling his target, he would be paid at the rate of 7.1 per cent of the adjusted gross margin of what he sells (£126,000 x 7.1 per cent = £8,940. Short by £60, but who's perfect?). If he meets his target of £126,000, he would receive the full £9,000. If he falls short, he is paid 7.1 per cent of what he sells.

A bonus of £1,500 (5 per cent of compensation) would be paid if the salesman achieved his sales target. A portion of the bonus might be payable on a lesser achievement, say £500 for making 90 per cent of target, £1,000 for 95 per cent.

Bonuses in all categories may be paid on a progressive basis, that is, increased for achievement in excess of target. For example, a salesman is paid a combined commission and bonus of 13.1 per cent on adjusted gross margin in excess of target.

Application of the Reward Scheme

We'll assume our hypothetical salesman has an adjusted gross margin target of £126,000 which he exceeds by £21,000. His target for opening new accounts is 48, but he fails to meet it, securing only 34 new customers. The sales manager reaches the conclusion the salesman has done a creditable job of working with new men and is entitled to the bonus for fulfilling his obligation in that area.

His earnings for the year would break down as illustrated in the table below.

I'm sure an alert sales manager would point out to the salesman that his failure to secure an additional 14 new accounts cost him £1,500, more than £100 an account.

The subjective judgement of the sales manager is called into play in only

		Totals
Training new men		
Salary	£3,000	
Bonus	1,500	
		£4,500
Opening new accounts		
Salary	1,500	
Bonus	—	1,500
Merchandising work, etc.		
Salary	3,000	3,000
Sales		
Salary	9,000	
Commission	9,000	
Bonus	1,500	
		19,500
		£28,500
Commission and bonus on £21,000 sales in excess of target at 13.1 per cent		2,751
Total Reward		£31,251

two areas: training new men and merchandising, promotional and servicing work. Only in the case of training duties is a bonus involved. The sales manager should possess enough evidence to make an informed judgement on the performance of any one of his men. He knows how many new men were assigned to a salesman for training and how many days he spent with them. He should also be in a position to know how effective their training has been.

No bonus is offered in the area of merchandising. If the sales manager feels the salesman has been neglecting his responsibilities in the area, he has all the authority he needs to call the salesman in and tell him what he expects of him in the future. After all, salary bases can be changed, and if a man is paid to do a job it should be done.

Benefits to be Derived from a Reward Scheme

Both the salesman and the company should profit handsomely from a well-designed and well-administered reward scheme similar to the one used in the example.

The salesman will enjoy the stability and security, of a substantial salary and will have a full understanding of the company's expectations of him. There will be a strong incentive for the salesman to achieve and even exceed his target. Since the adjusted gross margin on his sales rose to £147,000, he is paid a combined commission and bonus of 13.1 per cent on the excess of £21,000. I am sure that next year he will not allow a shortage of a few new accounts to cost him a bonus of £1,500.

The company maintains full control over its men. A sales manager need not be reluctant to advise or instruct a man who receives more than half his pay in the form of salary. The sales manager will be able continually to monitor the performance of a man throughout the year. He will even have the means to encourage his men to make required reports; how can a salesman expect to earn a portion of his salary for promotional work if he doesn't let the boss know what he has been doing in that direction?

A well-designed and well-controlled scheme will do much to aid a company in meeting its selling goals.

General Discussion of Schemes

The scheme can be used for any level of earnings target. At a £20,000 target, each point would be worth £200, and at £40,000 twice that. Naturally, a company would exert great care in picking the components of its scheme. In certain circumstances, opening new accounts might be weighted more heavily. Should all territories be well-manned and little expansion planned, training new men would be relatively unimportant.

In situations where sales are highly technical in nature, reward would lean even more heavily on salary and less on commission. On the other hand, companies finding it essential to increase sales would provide salesmen greater incentive by relying more heavily on commission and a generous bonus. Other companies with a narrow line of products, all carrying basically the same gross margin, might base commission on gross sales volume instead of on gross margin or adjusted gross margin. Still other companies, striving even harder to increase sales, could adopt a progressive commission schedule as targets are met or surpassed.

In short, every company has the means to tailor its reward scheme to its needs.

All men are not £30,000 a year men. The sales manager is responsible for evaluating the potential of the individuals in his sales force. In the example we picked a man who, in the estimation of the sales manager, should earn £30,000. Perhaps the next man on the list happens to be relatively new, not yet fully experienced, but definitely on the way up. In the past year he earned £21,000 and the sales manager is convinced he could reach £24,000 to £25,000 in the current year. On that salesman's chart, a point would be valued at £250. Naturally, his sales target would be compatible with the earnings target.

What I am saying is that flexibility is the key in any reward scheme. It's the responsibility of the sales manager to make correct judgements about his sales force.

Company Preferences in Reward Schemes

There are statistics galore relating to company and industry preferences for various reward schemes. The one thing they have in common is their age when published. However, attitudes toward reward do not change overnight and a tardy statistical approach is better than no approach at all.

Roughly speaking, a quarter of companies pay straight salary to salesmen. Another fourth pay a combination of salary and commission. Almost a third pay a combination of salary and individually earned bonus. The balance use various mixtures involving salary, commission, group bonus, advances and whatever else strikes their fancy.

Almost all the experts tell us in no uncertain terms that it is the responsibility of the sales manager to keep selling costs to as small a percentage of sales volume as possible. Curiously, they talk very little about his responsibility in the area of selling. In my opinion the sales manager's major responsibility is to get out of his territory as many sales as he can through legitimate and ethical methods. He is, of course, interested in holding down costs, but not to the point that men are not paid in fair proportion to their performance. No one should want to pay £2 for an item worth £1, but no intelligent person tries to get something for nothing.

Classification of Salesmen

Any effective reward scheme must offer a just reward for services rendered. Every scheme must start with an evaluation of each person on the sales force. Some companies classify men in groups, say A, B, C, and D. Criteria for inclusion in a group might be:

1. Age
2. Experience
3. Potential
4. Past record of earnings

New, inexperienced men would start as class D and move up as their performance improved. If they didn't improve after a reasonable period, changes would have to be made.

The middle groups would include, in addition to the men moving up, those nearing retirement who might have been transferred to more compact, mature territories. A substantial portion of Bs and Cs would be men of limited potential who can be relied on to do adequate, but unremarkable jobs. This segment might very well be the backbone of the entire organization — uninspired but loyal, hard-working individuals. Don't ever discount their contributions.

Members of group A are the tigers of every sales force. They produce, how they do produce. They can be and often are difficult to handle and get along with. Controlling them turns sales managers' hair grey and begets ulcers. But what do sales managers expect in return for their pay?

Companies using the group system might set it up like this:

Group	*Rewarding range*
A	£25,000 to £50,000
B	£22,000 to £27,000
C	£18,000 to £24,000
D	£14,000 to £19,000

Salaries, sales targets, bonuses and so forth would be set up to conform. Again, the key to success is the sales manager's ability to assess the abilities of his force and arrive at a realistic estimate of the expected earnings of his men.

Can a Salesman Be Paid Too Much?

Of course a salaried salesman can be paid too much, especially if his father happens to be the chairman of the board. I'm not talking about him or the fortunate chap who profits from a once-in-a-lifetime windfall or bonanza.

I am talking about those few marvellous producers in whose hands customer after customer becomes a gold mine. Should a ceiling be placed on such a man's earnings? Here again I differ from those pundits who advance the same old arguments that recommend denial of commission on windfalls and approve the theory of regressive commission rates to limit earnings. They recommend a ceiling be placed on rewards, that bonuses of top producers be cut. They suggest that salary be raised almost to selected earnings limits and commission and bonus be practically eliminated.

I approve none of these actions. When the same experts preach the theory that it is wrong to pay a salesman more than his sales manager to avoid undermining the manager's authority, demoralizing the manager and preventing top salesmen from aspiring to promotion to management, I shrug my shoulders and say, 'So what?'

It would appear that those authorities regard salesmen and management as adversaries. They seem to believe that it is the responsibility of the administration to pay not one cent more than it is forced to pay and that salesmen should be prevented from getting out of line and are not entitled to earn as much as their rightful superiors.

What can be the origin of such thinking? Isn't this still the land of opportunity where a man can go as far as his wit and ability can take him? I haven't once heard or read one of these advocates of repression state that a ceiling should be placed on what a man could sell provided the factory had no production problems. Heavens no. Let him sell as much as he can, just don't pay him.

And the adversary attitude bothers me. Isn't management on the same team as the salesman? Doesn't each depend on the efforts of the other to succeed or even to survive? Finally, the imposition of a ceiling on a salesman's earnings is totally foreign to the philosophy of selling.

When a sales manager has properly evaluated the potential of a territory using tested methods and a supremely endowed man makes mincemeat of his target, flooding the office with an unceasing spate of orders, why shouldn't he enjoy the fruits of his efforts? He isn't profiting at anyone's expense; the branch and the company share in his success. The sales manager receives a bonus and a profit-sharing cheque and the company profits increase once budget costs are met and incremental revenue rolls in.

Who loses? No one. Other salesmen have a wonderful example to emulate. The success of one man can be a strong motivating influence on an entire office. Profits come from sales made, not refused. Pay the man who makes them. A policy of paying lower commission rates on less profitable products is quite another matter and in many circumstances has much to recommend it.

Over-Rich Territories

Several writers on the subject suggest that if a salesman has extraordinary earnings, *ipso facto* his territory is too rich or too large and should be restructured. This could just possibly be the case. It is the responsibility of the sales manager to see that aberrations of this type are avoided.

On the other hand, if the resident salesman is actually doing the work of two men why should a change be made? What is involved is a matter of coverage. If a man is cleaning up by skimming a rich area, changes are in order. If he is getting a greater-than-expected share of the market in his area why upset the applecart? If the star performer is a one shot hot-shot his earnings will soon slide back to normal, but if he really is someone special his earnings will soar wherever he is stationed.

A theory is held that a man makes a territory, not the reverse. There is much evidence to support this attitude. When a £30,000 a year man in a 'poor' territory moves to a richer one it often happens that within a short period of time he will again be earning at his historic rate. Conversely, a man averaging £20,000 a year who is transferred to a 'good' territory might show a short-term spurt in earnings, but will soon relapse to his normal earnings level. This phenomenon does not occur in every case, but it occurs often enough to support a suspicion that a man has an inclination to maintain his earnings level irrespective of where he is assigned.

It is the function of sales management to match the right man to the right territory. Perhaps a sales manager's greatest pleasure and satisfaction comes when he is able to convert a £20,000 a year man into a £30,000 earner. Yes, there is some joy in a sales manager's life and the good ones rejoice when they are able to lead a man and his family into a better standard of living. That's success and that's what it's all about.

Introduction of the Scheme

This is probably the most sensitive element of the whole process of developing and installing a reward scheme. It is a human instinct to resist change and resistance grows in direct proportion to the importance of what is changed. Reward management must stand very high on a salesman's priority list.

All organizations, especially large ones, would be wise to pretest a district for a year before installing a new system throughout the company, provided it represents a major change from a previous system. A careful analysis should be made of the immediately past period and reward figured under the new scheme for each salesman. If application of the new scheme would have resulted in substantial variation from what was actually paid, the cause of the aberration should be determined and a judgement made whether the difference was justifiable.

If the application of the new scheme would have resulted in generally lower rewards, a revision of elements would probably be in order. If payments would have been generally higher for approximately the same work done, it is equally reasonable to seek the cause and, if justified, make revisions.

Some differences between the old and the new scheme would be expected. If rewards under both schemes were the same, why make changes? The new scheme would have been designed with three purposes in mind: to relate reward with contribution, to provide incentive to salesmen to achieve even more and to enable the company to point the sales force's efforts in directions more advantageous to the company. To put it another way, the new scheme should make it possible for a salesman to do better for himself by focusing his efforts in areas more profitable to his employer.

For example, a company might weigh a scheme in a direction that would correct a weakness in its marketing strategy. The shift from gross volume to adjusted gross margin as a commission base should be a powerful incentive to a salesman to sell the more profitable of the company products. The effect of such a shift in salesman motivation should not be neglected when projecting earnings under the new system and comparing them with the results for the previous year under the old scheme.

Let us spend another minute or two on this change. The salesman who had in the past sold a large percentage of high-margin products would profit through the new system. Conversely, the man who had concentrated on high-volume, low margin items would do worse. One salesman would be happy with the new arrangement, the other wouldn't.

Yet, the individual who contributed the most to the success of the company would be more highly rewarded for his efforts and the other chap, for his own benefit as well as that of the company, would do well to revise his selling habits. The company might with justification say that one man had been underpaid, the other overpaid and the change in commission base was made to correct the imbalance. To make an omelette one must crack a few eggs.

Motivation and incentive are the keys. Give a salesman a reason for doing what is best for him. The company will profit automatically if the salesman meets the goals set for him.

Presentation of the Scheme

Let us assume our sales manager has done his homework thoroughly and is ready to proceed with the installation of the new scheme in his district, the one picked by the company for the test. How does he go about it? Does he send a circular to each of the eight men involved in the change announcing that on January 1, three weeks from now, a new reward scheme will be introduced? Does he add a short paragraph to the effect that if every salesman puts his shoulder to the wheel for the next year, he will find that the new scheme is better for him than the old one? I am afraid that some unenlightened sales managers would do just that.

On the other hand, a top quality sales manager goes about the introduction of a new scheme quite differently. Well in advance of the change-over date he has:

1. Analysed all his facts and figures for the eight men in his office, including earnings to date (say through November 30) figured on the old and new basis.
2. Prepared targets for the next year for the entire force.
3. Projected earnings for each man based on recommended areas of concentration. More effort and attention here, less there.
4. Prepared a presentation for the announcement. When the sales manager prepares, he should really prepare. He is aware that, at least at the beginning of his presentation, he will have an unfriendly audience. Every man will resist change. A few will control their reactions and keep a relatively open mind, and their attitude will at best be one of wary scepticism. They will hear the sales manager out before they make a judgement, but he knows if he doesn't have a good story, they will join the others who are already convinced that any change the company makes is designed for the sole purpose of cutting their earnings.

   In making his presentation the sales manager will not discuss particulars about any of his men. He will explain the scheme in general terms, showing how each element fits into the whole. His experience has taught him another important fact not to be ignored when talking to his men in a group. That is to leave company interests out of his presentation as much as possible. Salesmen worry about themselves. Their attitude is that the company has any number of people looking after its interests while no one is really going to bat for them.

Our particular sales manager has good rapport with his men. He has always treated them fairly and they do respect him, that is why his district was chosen for the test. But he also knows his men won't take him entirely on trust. He must prove that the new scheme, properly used, will benefit them.

5. Rehearsed his presentation to assure it will be clear, concise and convincing. He will record and play back successive efforts until he is satisfied the final product can be improved no further.

The sales manager calls his men in and introduces the scheme. At the end of his presentation he announces that within the week he will discuss with each man how the change will affect him.

The order of these meetings is of considerable importance. The sales manager has been sensitive to the reaction of each man during his presentation. It is not difficult for him to read the expressions and attitudes he observes. The salesman scheduled for the first meeting will be a loyal and successful company man whose attitude during the presentation indicated that he was amenable to change or at least not strongly opposed. The last man on the schedule has a reputation for opposing anything that comes along.

If a good job has been done in setting up the schedule and the manager handles each man with tact and demonstrates how the scheme can be an advantage if the salesman adjusts to it, he will find public opinion swinging over to his side. Grapevines in sales organizations are well organized and fully knowledgeable. That is why the schedule was organized as it was.

The manager will, wherever possible, arrange for meetings to take place in the salesman's territory, where he will be more comfortable than in the district office.

Once the scheme is introduced and in operation, the job is not finished. The manager must be alert to handle any snags that develop. He must keep his ear fine-tuned to the continuing reactions of his men. He must also be aware to what extent each man is or is not using the scheme to his advantage. The sales manager has been around long enough to know that if the salesmen are content and prosperous the company can't help but do well. Its profits derive from the success of its men. Make them successful and everyone wins.

And now, to wrap up what I have to say, a few suggestions.

Hints to Sales Managers

- Realize that your men are real people, just like yourself, not inanimate pieces to be pushed around on a chess board.
- You speak of 'your men', 'your sales force'. If they are truly yours, you have a responsibility to ensure they always receive every consideration due them.
- Salesmen and the companies they represent are not adversaries; they both pursue the same goal — success — and to achieve it each must place full faith and confidence in the other.
- Match reward as closely as possible with contribution.
- Earn the respect of your men. Show them the respect they richly deserve.

Chapter 14

A SALES MANAGER'S RESPONSE TO PROBLEMS

There are signals that should alert a perceptive sales executive to the need for revision in his company's reward scheme. Telltale symptoms will also surface when territories require restructuring or when the traditional method of market coverage whether it be through employee salesmen, manufacturer's reps or distributors, should be changed. We'll devote the final few pages of this book to a discussion of how a sales manager can spot trouble areas and the actions he can take once they have been pinpointed.

Faulty reward schemes can be held at least partially to blame when:

1. Morale is low in a sales force. Men and women start to grumble. Nothing quite suits them; they bicker with management and among themselves. Some individuals feel that they are underpaid while others are grossly overpaid.
2. Customer complaints increase. Service obligations are neglected and salesmen's attitudinal problems are brought to the attention of management.
3. Turnover in the sales force increases. The warning flag really waves when long-time, steady producers begin to seek other employment.
4. It becomes increasingly difficult to hire qualified replacements.
5. Sales decrease, share of market declines.
6. Salesmen's earnings do not keep pace with industry averages.
7. The number of accounts closed exceeds the number of new ones opened.
8. The sales manager begins to realize he is losing rapport with his men. An adversary relationship rears its ugly head.

The list of danger signals is by no means complete, but does cover the basic indicators that portend imminent collapse of a sales force. No perceptive sales manager would wait until a half-dozen warning bells rang before going into action. His fine-tuned ear would pick up the first rumblings of unrest in his organization and he would take immediate steps to correct the situation.

The first move would be the most distasteful to him; it would also be the most important. He would examine, honestly and objectively, his own actions and behaviour to determine whether they contributed in any way to the malaise of his organization. Has he been:

1. Fair and impartial in his dealings with his men and women, or has he been guilty of favouritism?
2. Supportive, or left his force to struggle along on its own?
3. Selfish or short-sighted when handling house accounts, unsolicited orders?
4. Truly interested in and concerned with the wellbeing of his people?
5. Fully on top of all aspects of his job?

Next he would question whether company policies were at fault.

1. Were policies reasonable and equitable to all salesmen, or slanted to the advantage of some and the disadvantage of others?
2. If a major portion of reward was salary, were amounts paid compatible with industry standards and were timely adjustments made in adequate amounts?
3. Were commission rates competitive?
4. Did the company reward scheme accurately relate reward with contribution?
5. Were territories constituted and assignments made so a man could achieve a level of earnings commensurate with his objectives?
6. Were territories allotted on a rational basis, or did company policy unfairly favour one class of salesman over another?
7. Were salesman's expenses fairly and adequately reimbursed?
8. Did company policies on windfalls, house accounts, returns, split commissions and so forth irritate the men to a marked extent?
9. Was the sales force kept in a state of constant confusion by an unending flow of seemingly unnecessary changes in company policies and standard operating procedures?
10. If earnings, and particularly bonuses, were based on achievement of targets, were they impartially and accurately fixed?
11. Did the reward scheme provide a strong incentive for men to do better for themselves?
12. Were earnings of salesmen in line with rewards paid by leading competitors?

The blunders of sales managers and weakness in company policies are the major causes of unrest in a sales force, but one other possible source of trouble cannot be ignored. I refer to the negative influence of a small group of salesmen, perhaps even a single individual. As a rotten apple can corrupt a whole barrel, so also can one disaffected salesman destroy the morale of an entire sales force. If such a person will not change his attitude he should be weeded out ruthlessly.

When the sales manager has isolated as far as possible the causes for discontent in his sales force, corrections should be made wherever needed. If the company reward scheme is the major culprit it should be reviewed, revised or discarded in favour of a scheme better suited to the needs of the sales force and the company.

Should a single salesman be dissatisfied with his territory, the matter is important but does not justify a wholesale overhaul of a district. Isolated situations should be handled when they arise, but if dissatisfaction with territorial assignments is rampant, the sales manager would act as he did in the previous example. He would first determine whether his actions had been responsible for the negative attitude of his men and women and then analyse the effect of company policies to discover whether they were to a degree culpable.

If territories and assignments had remained unchanged for a long period, he would probably find that substantial inequities would have developed and many of the complaints would be justified. Should such a situation arise, the sales manager should bear the major portion of the blame. It is his job to remain alert to what is going on in his district. He cannot be excused for failure to detect and act on inequities as they arise, preferably long before they reach the problem stage.

As we have stated earlier, territories change as men do. The matching process must continue unceasingly. Territories require redefinition: the objectives of some men rise as those of others fall. A major part of a sales manager's job is to monitor the performance of each of his men and to keep a close eye on the changes in the potential of each territory under his control. A competent sales manager:

1. Constantly reviews and refines his estimates or territorial potential.
2. Keeps a close check on the percentage of potential achieved in each territory.
3. Relates a salesman's earnings to share of potential attained in his territory.
4. Knows how salesmen's current earnings compare with previous averages. In cases of persistent or abrupt declines he will discover the reasons.
5. Is aware of a representative's performance with respect to his earnings target.
6. Knows what per cent of target each man will probably attain and the reason for superior or inferior performance.

His analysis will enable the sales manager to evaluate the performance of each of his men. He will know which are over-achieving, which are not performing as well as they should. He will recognize the individuals who have proved they can handle a richer territory and identify those on whom a superior territory is wasted.

He will also be aware of those territories that should be restructured: some divided to accommodate a second man, others broken up and segments added to adjoining territories.

He will recognize when the time is ripe to discontinue the use of manufacturer's reps or distributors in an area and cover it with company men. Conversely, he will be ready to shift to another method of marketing when an area becomes so poor it is no longer economic to continue normal coverage.

Forewarned is forearmed. A sales manager has no one to blame but himself if his sales force becomes disgruntled and, because of that, fails to meet the goals set for it. The only factors he cannot be held responsible for are declining economic conditions and the inability of the company to produce an adequate supply of quality merchandise to sell. Everything else falls in his lap.

He shouldn't even be allowed to place the blame for problems in his district on short-sighted company policies, even if they are principally responsible for the deteriorating situation. If policies are at fault, it is his obligation to demonstrate the fact and continue his crusade for correction until it is successful.

Harsh words? Perhaps so. A tough job being a sales manager? No argument there, but look at it this way: Selling is a noble profession and a sales executive is in a unique position where his efforts can have a major influence in several areas. Success in handling his job means that customer needs are adequately served, his company prospers and all the men and women in his organization or under his leadership have ample opportunity to achieve whatever goals they set for themselves.

You will always have problems. Handle them, but keep your eyes fixed firmly on the rewards that accompany successful performance of your duties.

INDEX